ON GOLDEN POND

BY **ERNEST THOMPSON**

★ Revised Edition

★

DRAMATISTS
PLAY SERVICE
INC.

For my parents, Esther and Theron Thompson,
who are not Ethel and Norman Thayer
but might be. With love and great admiration.

INTRODUCTION

ON GOLDEN POND has been produced in forty countries, in three Broadway houses and in theatres all across America; it was made into a movie, for which I won an Academy Award; I wrote and directed a musical version and a live television production, starring Julie Andrews and Christopher Plummer; and, after all that, I'm still trying to get it right. While the play, like any work of art, is about many things, what I thought I was writing as a young man was a study in dysfunction, one family's struggles with what we all struggle with — age, rage, regret, love withheld, love unspoken, disappointment and, ultimately, if we're lucky, forgiveness, acceptance and renewal. Maybe it's because it's so funny, or because there's so much emotion in the piece, but there's a tendency sometimes to make the play softer and sweeter than intended. When we revived it on Broadway with James Earl Jones, the director, Leonard Foglia, and I made it our goal to make ON GOLDEN POND as unsentimental and unflinching as I had originally conceived it. It wasn't the actors' skin color that made the production significant; it was the courage of their performances, not to yield to the tenderness, but to keep the tension real, and, in the process, the stakes high. As a consequence, it was far and away the funniest production I've ever been associated with, the humor coming from the same painful place it does in real life, and, based on the handkerchiefs and the delicious silences, the play was just as moving as ever. This is that production's script, the same story I wrote as a twenty-eight-year-old man, augmented by a line or two stolen from the film or the musical. James Earl was the first actor I'd ever had ask what was being said on the other end of the telephone, so I wrote it for him. You may, of course, choose to leave it to the performers' imaginations, but I have included the lines regardless. Also, a number of words in the script appear in brackets. You may find it helpful to update these words with more contemporary references. If so, please ensure that any updates conform to the spirit of the originals. Enjoy your time on the lake.

ON GOLDEN POND was first presented by The Hudson Guild Theatre (Craig Anderson, Producing Director; David Kerry Heefner, Associate Director; Harold Sogard; Managing Director) at The Hudson Guild Theatre in New York City, opening on September 13, 1978, for a limited run of 36 performances. It was directed by Craig Anderson; the set design and costume design were by Steven Rubin; the lighting design was by Craig Miller; and the production stage manager was Daniel Morris. The cast was as follows:

NORMAN THAYER, JR. .... Tom Aldredge
ETHEL THAYER .... Frances Sternhagen
CHARLIE MARTIN .... Ronn Carroll
CHELSEA THAYER WAYNE .... Zina Jasper
BILLY RAY .... Mark Bendo
BILL RAY .... Stan Lachow

ON GOLDEN POND was subsequently produced by The Hudson Guild Theatre (Craig Anderson, Producer) and presented by Arthur Cantor and Greer Garson at the New Apollo Theatre in New York City, opening on February 28, 1979. It was directed by Craig Anderson; the set design and costume design were by Steven Rubin; and the lighting design was by Craig Miller.

NORMAN THAYER, JR. .... Tom Aldredge
ETHEL THAYER .... Frances Sternhagen
CHARLIE MARTIN .... Ronn Carroll
CHELSEA THAYER WAYNE .... Barbara Andres
BILLY RAY .... Mark Bendo
BILL RAY .... Stan Lachow

CHARACTERS

NORMAN THAYER, JR.

ETHEL THAYER

CHARLIE MARTIN

CHELSEA THAYER WAYNE

BILLY RAY

BILL RAY

SETTING

The living room of a summer home
on Golden Pond, in Maine.

ON GOLDEN POND

ACT ONE

Scene 1

The middle of May. Early afternoon.

The setting is the living room of a summer home on Golden Pond, in Maine. The room is large and old and high ceilinged, all wood and glass, not sparkling like a picture in House Beautiful, but rich and wrinkled and comfortable-looking. The house was built in 1914, as a plaque on the chimney proclaims, and it has aged well. Its beams and plank walls are a deep brown, window sills and doorways fading green, hooked rugs and plaid curtains still bright. There is a line of windows upstage, the sort that can be cranked open, with screens on the outside. Through them can be seen trees, and then a brightness because the sun is reflecting on the lake down below. If one looked far enough, one could see mountains in the distance. And that is all. Just a house on the lake in the woods.

There is a heavy paneled door up right, open now, showing a screen door beyond it, and an outside porch beyond that, a platform really with several outdoor chairs sitting on it. In the left corner upstage a stairway leads to a landing where there is a closed door, and then bends and rises higher still, disappearing into a hallway. The upstage area of the room is raised by two or three steps. In the right corner is a tall folding glass door, closed now, and beyond it a dining area, an old oak table with chairs piled on it's top. The stage right wall is dominated by a huge fieldstone fireplace with a wide slab hearth. On either side there are wood boxes with plaid cushions, and, above them, shelves and shelves of books and games and knickknacks and more books, rising all the way to the ceiling. Stage left there is another, smaller table, chairs upside down on it, too, and there are two doors, both closed. The upstage one is the swinging variety, and the entrance to the kitchen, the downstage door leads outside. A little window beside it shows a bit of the shingled back porch and more trees.

The room is a trifle disorganized. Its furniture, a fat couch, and two fat chairs, two rockers by the fireplace, are all covered with dust cloths. A chair by the entrance door has a footstool overturned in its lap, and, next to it, a small table holding a fifties-style telephone. There are other tables, curious hand-made relics, clustered in the center of the room waiting to go outside. The rugs are all rolled up. There are floor lamps here and there, end tables, hassocks, a basket of wood, bric-a-brac galore, fishing poles in a rack, anchors, pine cones, boat cush-ions, and the like. A row of old hats and a pair of binoculars hang from hooks upstage. Everything looks as though it's been there forever, and while the room is cluttered it still looks like a nice place to curl up and take a nap. Everywhere, on the wall and on the mantel, on the bookshelves and window sills, on the tables and the doors, are pictures, photographs, most of them framed, most of them old and brown, some new. Pictures of people, groups, families, children, animals, places, the whole room a huge photo album, a huge book of memories.

When the curtain rises there is a quiet for a moment, and then footsteps can be heard in the hall upstairs. Norman Thayer, Jr., appears on the steps. He is 79. He wears baggy pants and sneakers and a sweater. His hair is white. He wears glasses. He walks slowly but upright. On the one hand he is boyish and peppery, having hung onto his vigor and his humor, but at the same time, he is grand, he has a manner, a way of speaking and of carrying himself.

He stands on the landing, taking in the room. He smiles. He walks down to the raised platform and stops at the entrance door. He stares out at the lake. He pushes the screen door, but instead of opening, it falls over. Norman watches it smack down onto the porch. He considers it a moment, then he turns and faces the room again. He steps to the phone and lifts the receiver. He listens. He calls offstage.

NORMAN. The phone works! *(He waits for an answer. There isn't one. He speaks to himself.)* At least I think it does. *(He returns the receiver to its cradle. He stares at the phone. After a moment he picks it up again and listens. He squints and dials "0." He listens. A moment passes.)* Hello? ... hello? *(His attention is diverted by a photo propped up on the mantel in front of him. He squints at it.)* Who the hell is that? *(He calls offstage.)* Who the *hell* is in this picture here? *(Hearing a voice now in the phone.)* Hello? Who is this?

THE OPERATOR. This is the operator.

NORMAN. The operator! What do you want?

THE OPERATOR. I beg your pardon?

NORMAN. You called, you must want something.

THE OPERATOR. You called me, sir.

NORMAN. But that was a long time ago. You never answered.

THE OPERATOR. We get a little busy.

NORMAN. I see. Well, here you are. How *are* you?

THE OPERATOR. Great.

NORMAN. How nice. Listen, this is Norman Thayer, Jr., Professor Emeritus, University of Pennsylvania, Department of English, over on Golden Pond.

THE OPERATOR. Where are you?

NORMAN. *Golden Pond.*

THE OPERATOR. And where is that?

NORMAN. It's in New England, dear, in the state of Maine.

THE OPERATOR. Where exactly?

NORMAN. Where are you?

THE OPERATOR. I'm in Waterville.

NORMAN. I thought so. You have the accent, you know.

THE OPERATOR. Doesn't sound like it to me.

NORMAN. Well, it doesn't matter. Golden Pond is very near wherever you are.

THE OPERATOR. Okey dokey.

NORMAN. I have something I would like you to do, if you could: Call me up. Can you do that?

THE OPERATOR. Is there some *reason* I'm doing it?

NORMAN. I want to check my phone and make certain it rings. It hasn't been rung all winter, that we know of; it may have lost its

9

whatsie.

THE OPERATOR. We'll give it a test then?

NORMAN. Thank you, dear. Do you have my number?

THE OPERATOR. We would need that.

NORMAN. Well, I should think you would.

THE OPERATOR. You could just read it to me. It's written on the phone.

NORMAN. What do you mean, written on the phone? There's nothing written on the phone. *(Staring at the dial.)* Oh, wait a minute. I see what you mean. But I can't make it out. *(He bends closer.)* Nope. Sorry. Too small. They should write the numbers bigger. You'll just have to look it up, dear.

THE OPERATOR. What's the exchange?

NORMAN. I haven't a clue. It has a nine in it, that's all I know.

THE OPERATOR. There's a lot of numbers with nines in them.

NORMAN. Yes, I suppose there *are* a lot of numbers with nines. Well, it's in the book. You must have a book. Norman Thayer, Jr. In the state of Maine.

THE OPERATOR. I'll call you back.

NORMAN. Fine. Thank you very much. *(He hangs up. He stares at the phone expectantly. Nothing happens. He puts his hand on the receiver in anticipation. A moment passes. Once again he squints at the photo.)* Who the hell is that? *(Now there comes a pounding on the downstage door. Norman is startled. He stares for a moment. The knock is repeated. Norman calls offstage.)* Someone's at the door!

ETHEL. It's me, you poop! *(Norman steps to the door and opens it. And in walks Ethel Thayer. Still pretty at sixty-nine and energetic beyond belief, she is Norman's opposite in many ways. She fills the empty spaces when he grows quiet. She knows how to manage his moods and run interference when he's less than charming with others. Dressed now in old jeans and jacket, she marches in, carrying a basket of branches.)*

NORMAN. Look at you.

ETHEL. Yes. Quite a sight, aren't I?

NORMAN. Where have you been?

ETHEL. In the woods.

NORMAN. In the woods. How nice.

ETHEL. Oh! It's *beautiful!* Everything's just waking up. Little tiny birds, little tiny leaves. I saw three chippies, and a whole patch of little tiny flowers out by the old cellar hole. And millions and millions of little tiny black flies. In my eyes and hair. Just Terrible!

NORMAN. What were you doing out there in the woods?

ETHEL. Getting kindling. *(She sets it on the hearth. She smiles at him, and then looks about the room.)* Just look at this place.

NORMAN. It's a mess, isn't it?

ETHEL. Not really. Just take a minute and it'll be all shipshape again. Come on. Help me with the dust covers. What's happened to the screen door?

NORMAN. It fell over.

ETHEL. How?

NORMAN. I pushed it.

ETHEL. What do you mean?

NORMAN. I pushed the door and the door fell over.

ETHEL. It's not supposed to do that when you push it.

NORMAN. I didn't think so. I'll fix it later.

ETHEL. You might have closed the big door.

NORMAN. Didn't want to touch it. I was afraid of what might happen.

ETHEL. Well, now we'll be swatting at black flies for the next two days. *(She closes the door.)* The room is probably full of them.

NORMAN. *(Looking about.)* I don't see any.

ETHEL. You *don't* see them till it's too late. *(She stares out the window.)* Of course they're never quite as bad on the lake side. Not when the wind blows. Whitecaps today.

NORMAN. Ah.

ETHEL. *(Crossing back down and beginning another dust cover.)* I met a very nice couple.

NORMAN. What? Where?

ETHEL. In the woods.

NORMAN. You met a couple in the woods? A couple of people? *(He is neatly folding his dust cover.)*

ETHEL. No, a couple of antelope. Of course a couple of people. You needn't be too careful with that. I'm going to hang them on the line anyway.

NORMAN. Oh. *(He thinks about it for a moment and then continues folding it.)* What were these people doing in the woods?

ETHEL. Walking. Their name was Melciorri, I think, or something.

NORMAN. Melciorri? What sort of name is that?

ETHEL. I don't know, dear. Italian, probably. They're up from Boston.

NORMAN. Ohhh. They speak English?

ETHEL. Tsk. Of course they speak English. How do you suppose

11

I talked to them? *(Lifting a dust cover.)* Here, help me with this. They're a very nice middle-aged couple. Just like us.

NORMAN. *(Dropping his own dust cover and taking an end of hers.)* If they're just like us, they're not middle-aged.

ETHEL. Of course they are.

NORMAN. Middle age means the middle, Ethel. The middle of life. People don't live to be 150.

ETHEL. We're at the far edge of middle age, that's all.

NORMAN. We're not, you know. We're not middle-aged. You're old, and I'm ancient.

ETHEL. Pooh. You're in your seventies and I'm in my sixties.

NORMAN. Just barely on both counts.

ETHEL. Are we going to spend the afternoon quibbling about this?

NORMAN. We can if you'd like.

ETHEL. *(Picking up another cover.)* The Melciorris, whatever their age group, are a nice couple, that's all. They're staying up at the Putnams', while the Putnams are in Europe.

NORMAN. Do the Putnams know about this?

ETHEL. Yes. They're the best of friends. That's what Mrs. Melciorri said.

NORMAN. Ha!

ETHEL. Oh, Lord. They've invited us for dinner, if we like.

NORMAN. Oh. Well. I'm not sure my stomach is ready for rigatoni and that sort of thing. Tiramisu.

ETHEL. We didn't discuss the menu. Want to help me with the rugs? Guess whom else I ran into.

NORMAN. You ran into someone else? The woods are full of people.

ETHEL. It was only Charlie.

NORMAN. Who's Charlie?

ETHEL. *Charlie.* The mailman.

NORMAN. Oh. What was Charlie the mailman doing in the woods?

ETHEL. He was on the road.

NORMAN. Oh. You went on the road, too. You didn't say that. You said you were in the woods. *(They unroll the rugs, Norman barely helping.)*

ETHEL. Well, the road goes through the woods, you know.

NORMAN. Of course it does.

ETHEL. Charlie wants to put in our dock.

NORMAN. What for?

ETHEL. To park the boat beside.

NORMAN. I'll put in the dock.

ETHEL. You *won't* put in the dock.

NORMAN. Why not?

ETHEL. Because you're too old.

NORMAN. I'm not old at all. I'm middle-aged.

ETHEL. Old Pearson's been putting in the dock for God knows how long anyway, but he died this past winter, so Charlie has offered to do it, now that Pearson has received his just reward.

NORMAN. How did that come about?

ETHEL. I don't know. I suppose he got ill.

NORMAN. No, how did the subject of our dock come about?

ETHEL. We started talking about the dock because Charlie said it would be two more weeks before he'd start delivering the mail by boat, and he wanted to be sure we were okay. He must be the busiest man in the state of Maine.

NORMAN. I should think so. Certainly the dimmest-witted.

ETHEL. Norman. *(She finds a cloth and begins to dust.)*

NORMAN. I remember Charlie when he was just a little fellow.

ETHEL. Yes.

NORMAN. Little blond-haired kid. Used to laugh at anything. I thought then that he was a bit deficient. Charlie must be thirty by now.

ETHEL. Charlie is forty-four. Two years older than Chelsea.

NORMAN. Chelsea is forty-two? Our Chelsea?

ETHEL. 'Fraid so.

NORMAN. Good God. *(He stands by the door, studying the rack of hats. He takes down an old straw one and puts it on. He admires himself in a small mirror that hangs by the door. Ethel strains to lug a handcrafted antique table.)* What do you think?

ETHEL. Quite a sight.

NORMAN. I should say so. How's that table, a bit heavy?

ETHEL. *(Noting that he's not helping.)* Yes. My father built this table. It's practically as old as the house. *(She sets it by the couch.)*

NORMAN. Your *father made* that?

ETHEL. *(Slightly annoyed.)* Yes. The first summer I went to Camp Koochakiyi. *(Rhymes with Pooch-a-bye-bye. Norman replaces the hat and dons a new one, a floppy red fishing hat. He checks himself out again.)* Charlie says he doesn't expect Miss Appley to make it up this year.

NORMAN. Who is Miss Appley?

ETHEL. Miss *Appley,* Norman, who lives with Miss Tate.

NORMAN. Ohhh. How do you like this one?

ETHEL. Stunning. They're both in their nineties, I should think. They were up here together when I was a teenager. Wearing their neckties and singing in the gazebo, holding hands. What a marvelous love affair. Can you imagine being together for so long?

NORMAN. No.

ETHEL. *(She throws the pile of dust clothes into the kitchen.)* Thanks a lot. Charlie says Miss Appley is just too frail, and Miss Tate won't come without her. One of them has a nephew, I believe, who'll get the house. It's sad, isn't it? *(She bends over and retrieves a wooden doll that has fallen onto the hearth.)* Oh, poor Elmer has had a terrible fall.

NORMAN. Who's poor Elmer?

ETHEL. *Elmer. (She holds up the doll.)* My doll. He fell in the fireplace.

NORMAN. Oh.

ETHEL. Poor little Elmer. The life you've had. *(To Norman.)* Did you know he turned sixty-five this spring?

NORMAN. No, I must say I wasn't aware of that.

ETHEL. I got him on my fourth birthday. I remember it quite clearly. I wanted a red scooter, but my father said red scooters were excessive and contrary to the ways of the Lord. He told me I'd understand when I was older. I'm a *lot* older now, and I'm afraid I still don't understand. But, he gave me Elmer. And Elmer and I became the best of friends. The times we had. He was my first true love, you know.

NORMAN. There's no real need for you to review the vagaries of your youth. I've realized all along that I wasn't the first in line.

ETHEL. No, you were a rather cheap substitute for my darling Elmer. Sixty-five years old. It's hard to think of a doll as being old. He doesn't look much different than he did. A bit faded perhaps. He'd still be a delight to a small child. Chelsea used to love him. And now he's had a fall, poor dear.

NORMAN. Maybe he was trying to kill himself. Maybe he wants to be cremated. Probably got cancer or termites or something.

ETHEL. Would you please shut up? I swear you get more morbid every year.

NORMAN. Well, it wouldn't be a bad way to go, huh? A quick front flip off the mantel, a bit of a kick at the last minute, and land right in the fire. Nothing to it.

ETHEL. Are you hungry, Norman?

NORMAN. Nope. When my number's up, do that for me, would you? Prop me up on the mantel and point out which way is down. I may even shoot for a full gainer with a half twist.

ETHEL. Norman …

NORMAN. It's that little kick at the end I might have trouble with. You could get Charlie and hoist me back up again if I make a mess of it.

ETHEL. Norman …

NORMAN. Give me three tries and we'll go with the highest score. I'd be pretty well dead anyway after three full gainers with half twists, so if I haven't managed to hit the fire by the third go, you could just give me a bit of a nudge.

ETHEL. Norman, you really are becoming a nitwit, aren't you?

NORMAN. I think I'll have that written into the final instructions of my will. Let's call up that Jewish person in Wilmington and see how much he'd charge for a rewrite. You won't even need an urn. You can just shovel me out when I'm done and put me on your flowers. *(The phone rings.)* That's probably Mr. Shylock now. Wanting to know if one of us has pooped out yet.

ETHEL. Your fascination with dying is beginning to frazzle my good humor. *(The phone rings.)* Don't you have anything else to think about?

NORMAN. Nothing quite as interesting. *(The phone rings.)*

ETHEL. Well, what's stopping you? Why don't you just take your dive and get it over with? See what it's like.

NORMAN. And leave you alone with Elmer? You must be mad. I know all those widow stories. Do you suppose you're going to answer that phone?

ETHEL. Yes. *(She glowers at him and then crosses and lifts the receiver.)* Hello? … Hello? *(To Norman.)* There's no one there.

NORMAN. Ah Ha! See!

ETHEL. Hello?

OPERATOR. I'm here, I really am.

ETHEL. Oh, hello.

OPERATOR. Is this the Norman Thayer, Jr. residence?

ETHEL. Yes.

OPERATOR. Is Norman Thayer, Jr. there?

ETHEL. Just a moment, please. *(She holds the phone out.)* It's for you.

NORMAN. *(Stepping down to her.)* Who is it?

ETHEL. I don't know.

NORMAN. Not Saint Peter, is it? *(She shakes her head and point-*

edly sets the phone down, just out of his reach. She goes upstage and begins dusting windows as he lifts the handset.) Hello? Who is this?

OPERATOR. It's your operator.

NORMAN. *(To Ethel.)* It's the operator. *(Into the phone.)* What do you want?

OPERATOR. You asked me to call.

NORMAN. I don't think so. Oh, to check the ring, of course. I'd given up on you. Does it work?

OPERATOR. You tell me.

NORMAN. Yes, I guess it did ring here, come to think of it. That's why we picked up. So. Everything's all hunky dory then, huh?

OPERATOR. As far as I'm concerned.

NORMAN. Great. Thank you.

OPERATOR. Have a nice day.

NORMAN. I beg your pardon?

OPERATOR. Have a nice day.

NORMAN. Oh. *(He hangs up and turns to Ethel.)* She said, "Have a nice day." What a strange thing to say. What did she think I was going to do? Well, the phone works.

ETHEL. Good. What about these fish poles? Been through them this year?

NORMAN. No. I doubt that I'll be doing any fishing this time round.

ETHEL. All right.

NORMAN. Seems a shame to spend the money for a license.

ETHEL. All right.

NORMAN. You'd think they'd give it free to an old case like me. It's not as though I'd go out there and deplete the entire trout population or anything.

ETHEL. You always catch your share. You always have.

NORMAN. Well, that's all behind me now.

ETHEL. All right, Norman. *(He looks about. There is tension in the air. He looks at the photo on the mantel.)*

NORMAN. Who the *hell* is in this picture?

ETHEL. What picture?

NORMAN. This one. Here. Some fat woman with a little fat baby.

ETHEL. What? Oh. That's Millie's daughter Jane and her grandson. I can't remember his name.

NORMAN. Oh. Who's Millie?

ETHEL. *Millie,* Norman. Our next-door neighbor in Wilmington.

16

NORMAN. Oh, yes. So that's what her name is. Well, there's a certain family resemblance through the generations, isn't there? Everyone's fat. *(Ethel studies him, concerned. Norman deflects her look by picking up another photo.)* Look. Here's Chelsea on the swim team at school. She wasn't exactly thin.

ETHEL. She had a few fat years.

NORMAN. It's no wonder she couldn't do a back flip. No center of gravity.

ETHEL. Well, she tried, Norman.

NORMAN. Of course she did. I remember.

ETHEL. She only did it for you anyway. She only wanted to please you.

NORMAN. Yep.

ETHEL. Maybe this year we could persuade her to come and spend a few days. Wouldn't that be nice? *(A moment passes. Norman breaks the mood.)*

NORMAN. Feel like a quick game of Parcheesi?

ETHEL. Not right this minute.

NORMAN. Okay. *(Ethel goes about cleaning and opening windows.)* I guess you wouldn't be up for Monopoly either then, huh?

ETHEL. Tonight, Norman. *(She smiles.)* We've got the whole summer. The whole summer for you to try and win back the fortunes you lost to me last year.

NORMAN. Heh heh.

ETHEL. I hope you've thought about your tactics over the winter. *(She goes on with her work. He pulls down a book and settles into a chair.)*

NORMAN. Heh heh.

ETHEL. Pretty shoddy, some of those moves of yours.

NORMAN. Heh, heh

ETHEL. We've got the whole summer. It's so good to be home, isn't it?

NORMAN. *(Reading at last.)* Mmmm.

ETHEL. *(Quite loudly.)* Norman!

NORMAN. *(Dropping his book.)* What?

ETHEL. The loons, Norman! I've spotted the loons!

NORMAN. Where?

ETHEL. Get the glasses. My word! *(Norman fetches the binoculars from their hook and stands beside Ethel. He trains them on the lake.)* They're so lovely. Do you see them?

NORMAN. No. Oh. There they are. Oh, my goodness.

17

ETHEL. Aren't they lovely?

NORMAN. They're huge! I've never seen such big loons in my life

ETHEL. *(Looking at where he's aimed the binoculars.)* Those are boats, you poop. Come in closer. By the float.

NORMAN. *(Lowering the glasses.)* Oh. Those little things. Look at them swimming about.

ETHEL. Black and sleek. Lovely animals.

NORMAN. How wonderful.

ETHEL. A husband and a wife. I think they're looking at us.

NORMAN. Yes, they are.

ETHEL. Oh, Norman, they're nudging each other. They're talking.

NORMAN. Yes. But I can't make out what they're saying. Can you read beaks?

ETHEL. They're kissing is what they're doing.

NORMAN. How wonderful.

ETHEL. Mmmm. Do you realize this is our forty-eighth summer together, Norman? Our forty-eighth summer on Golden Pond.

NORMAN. Huh. *(After a moment.)* Probably our last.

ETHEL. Oh. Shut up.

Scene 2

The middle of June. Mid-morning. The setting is the same. There is a tablecloth on the oak table. The big door closed. The screen door is back in place. Norman is sitting at the dining table, studying the classified ads. After a moment he looks up and calls offstage.

NORMAN. Here's one. Listen. "Driver wanted for occasional chauffeuring and errands. Five days a week. Pay negotiable." Sound about right? *(He waits for an answer. There is none. He reads to himself.)* "Experience required." Well, I guess I've had experience. I've driven enough cars, God knows. *(He calls offstage.)* How many cars would you say I've had? *(No answer. He talks to himself.)* Twenty probably. If you don't count the [Nash]. Twenty cars and one [Nash]. Sounds like experience to me. *(He calls.)* I think I'll give these people a call. Huh? *(No answer. Then, to himself.)* There's no

18

number. How do you like that? For God's sake. It's so typical. They want a man for a job and yet they don't list the number. Well, I hope those errands weren't too crucial. Good God! *(He reads on. There is a knock on the door. Norman looks up, startled. He calls to the kitchen.)* Someone's at the door!

ETHEL. It's me, you poop! Open up! *(Norman opens the door. Ethel walks in, a bucket in each hand. Norman closes the door behind her.)*

NORMAN. What were you doing out there?

ETHEL. I was picking berries. There are oodles and oodles of little tiny strawberries along the old town road. Look.

NORMAN. *(Looking into the buckets.)* Ah. Very nice.

ETHEL. Unfortunately there are also oodles and oodles of mosquitoes. Worse this year than ever.

NORMAN. Really. I hadn't noticed them.

ETHEL. You've barely gone outside. What on earth you're doing in here on a day like today is beyond me.

NORMAN. Oh. Well. I've been quite busy. I've been looking through yesterday's paper for gainful employment. *(He crosses to his papers.)*

ETHEL. Here we go again. *(She exits to the kitchen. Norman doesn't notice her absence.)*

NORMAN. Very good prospects, I think. Chauffeurs, yardwork. The Dairy Divine wants an ice cream dipper. I think I could do something like that, don't you? *(He turns. She's not there.)* Oh. *(He looks about him. Ethel walks back into the room.)* Oh. There you are. What do you think?

ETHEL. I think this business of looking in the classified ads is about the silliest nonsense I've ever heard. What are you going to do if you call up and someone says, "Come on over and start tomorrow"?

NORMAN. Go on over and start tomorrow.

ETHEL. Oh, for the love of God. Whatever is the matter with you? Why don't you take a bucket and go pick us another quart of strawberries? I'll fix us up a scrumptious shortcake for lunch.

NORMAN. You want *me* to pick strawberries?

ETHEL. Yes. Do I have to put an ad in the paper?

NORMAN. I'm not sure I know how to pick strawberries.

ETHEL. There's really nothing to it, Norman. You bend over, and you pick them.

NORMAN. Bend over? Whatever for? Where are they?

ETHEL. They're on the ground, where they belong.

19

NORMAN. But, you've already filled the buckets.

ETHEL. Don't move. *(He doesn't. She exits into the kitchen. The sound of a motorboat can be heard. Norman looks to the lake.)*

NORMAN. Here comes whatshisname. He'll be bringing the paper, you know. I wouldn't want to miss any career opportunities just because I'm out looking for strawberries.

ETHEL. *(Coming back with an empty bucket.)* I'll pay you, Norman. It could be the beginning of something big. You may become a major strawberry picker.

NORMAN. Not if I have to be bending over all the time. I think you're trying to kill me.

ETHEL. I've thought about it.

NORMAN. You needn't bother. I'm on borrowed time as it is.

ETHEL. Would you please take your cheery personality and get out of here?

NORMAN. Maybe I could lie down to pick the berries.

ETHEL. Would you go on?

NORMAN. Where did you say these strawberries were? Other than on the ground I mean?

ETHEL. On the old town road. Just up from the meadow. *(He exits. Ethel watches him go. There's a look in her eyes, partly concern, partly pleasure at making old Norman get moving. She closes the door and crosses the room, tidies the pile of newspapers. The motor is very loud now. Ethel steps up onto the platform and looks down at the lake. She opens the wooden door and calls through the screen.)* Yoo hoo! Charlie! Hey! *(The motor stops.)* Good morning. Got some coffee on, if you'd like. Come on up, you can take five minutes off. I'll write you a note and you can send it to the Postmaster General. *(She steps quickly to the kitchen where she can be heard banging about. After a moment Charlie Martin appears on the porch. He's a big, round, blond-haired man, weather beaten face, smiling eyes, strong Maine accent. He is indeed a laugher, but not exactly "deficient." In his rustic, simple, thoughtful way, he is actually quite charming. He carries a small package, a rolled newspaper, and several letters. He peers through the screen door.)*

CHARLIE. Morning, Ethel.

ETHEL. *(Opening the kitchen door and leaning out.)* Come in, Charlie, and have a seat. Like a biscuit?

CHARLIE. Sure. *(She goes back inside. Charlie pulls the screen door. It falls back over on him. He wrestles with it and it slams down onto the porch.)* Uh oh. *(Ethel comes back out, having heard the noise.)* I

20

think I broke your door.

ETHEL. Oh, no. It's been that way for a month now. I should have warned you. Norman is supposed to fix it. It's not high on his list of priorities. I'm afraid.

CHARLIE. *(He sets down the mail and leans the door up against the wall.)* I could give it a try. It's just missing its little thing-amabobbers, that's all.

ETHEL. No, better let Norman get to it. Come in and let's close the big door before every mosquito in the county finds its way in here. *(He steps in, laughing, leaving the mail outside.)*

CHARLIE. Pretty bad this year, huh?

ETHEL. Worse than ever. Sit down. How's your brother? We haven't seen him at all this season.

CHARLIE. You mean Tom?

ETHEL. That's the only brother you have, isn't it?

CHARLIE. Yes. He's fine. He's just come back up from Portland. Got stopped twice for speeding. Once down and once up. *(He laughs.)* By the same policeman. *(He laughs. Ethel comes in with a coffee carafe.)* You should have seen his face.

ETHEL. I love your laugh, Charlie.

CHARLIE. Thank you. *(He laughs.)* Tom wasn't too happy to hear it yesterday. I don't know, it just struck me as awfully funny that he could be stupid enough to be stopped twice by the same cop. When he told me, I couldn't stop laughing. *(He laughs. He stops.)* Tom's not speaking to me anymore now. *(He helps himself to his coffee and grabs a biscuit. Ethel smiles at him.)* Where's Norman?

ETHEL. Norman is off picking strawberries. I threw him out. *(Charlie laughs.)* Don't laugh. *(Charlie stops.)* Norman is restless this year. I don't know what's got into him. How's your mother?

CHARLIE. *My* mother?

ETHEL. Yes.

CHARLIE. She's holding her own. *(He laughs and laughs.)* She fell down, you know, a couple of months ago.

ETHEL. I didn't know that.

CHARLIE. Yuh, a couple of months ago, right on her rump, when she was out helping clean up the town common with the Ladies' Auxiliary. She was having a tug-a-war with a dead juniper bush, and she won, or lost, depending on how you look at it. *(He laughs.)* She hasn't been normal since. *(He laughs.)* She walks all right, and sleeps and everything. She just can't sit. *(He snickers.)* It's taken a little adjustment. *(He laughs and laughs. Ethel smiles.)* If you'll pardon the expression, she's one old lady who really believes in busting her ass for the community. *(He howls. Ethel joins in, neither of them noticing at first as Norman steps in, carrying a bucket.)* Hi, Norman.

ETHEL. Hello, Norman. What are you doing back already? You've barely left.

NORMAN. So? I moved fast. I ran all the way, picked without stopping and ran all the way back.

ETHEL. *(Rising and starting to head him off.)* Well, I don't believe a word of it. Let me see what you've got.

NORMAN. I'll just dump them in with yours. Stay where you are.

ETHEL. *(Getting closer.)* Let me see.

NORMAN. No. I don't have many.

ETHEL. *(On him now. She reaches for the bucket.)* Just let me see. *(He tries to pull away. They wrestle with the bucket, it drops on the floor and bounces.)* There's nothing in it at all. You didn't get a single strawberry. What's the matter with you?

NORMAN. *(Looking at the empty bucket.)* I must have eaten them all.

ETHEL. Why didn't you stay and pick some?

NORMAN. Too many mosquitoes. You were right about them. I was afraid I'd contract malaria and die before my time.

ETHEL. Well, I don't know. Do you want some coffee?

NORMAN. No. *(He looks at Charlie.)* No mail today, Charlie?

CHARLIE. Holy Mackinoly! I left it on the porch!

NORMAN. Well, how about fetching it? Could you do that?

CHARLIE. You bet. *(He jumps up and goes out the door.)*

NORMAN. Look out for the mosquitoes.

ETHEL. You want a glass of milk, Norman?

NORMAN. No.

ETHEL. I'll get you one. *(She exits to the kitchen. Norman watches her go. He looks out at Charlie.)*

NORMAN. I see you broke the screen door, Charlie.

CHARLIE. *(Coming back in.)* Yuh, well, I think you need a couple of little thing-amabobbers for the hinges.

NORMAN. Oh, I don't know about that. It's been working all right. You must have yanked at it. Let's have the mail.

CHARLIE. Oh. Yuh. *(Holding it out.)* Got a package for you. *(Ethel comes back in with a glass of milk.)*

ETHEL. Here, Norman. Drink this. *(She hands it to him.)*

NORMAN. Thank you, nurse.

ETHEL. Sit down, Charlie.

CHARLIE. I should get going, I guess. Or somebody's not going to get their mail.

NORMAN. He's right, Ethel. Neither rain nor sleet nor hot biscuits, and all that.

ETHEL. Sit down, Charlie, and finish your coffee. *(Charlie hesitates and then sits by Norman. Ethel returns to her chair. Norman is wrestling with the package.)* What have you got there, Norman?

NORMAN. I have no idea, I can't open it. *(He passes it to Charlie.)* Here, could you bite this, please? *(Charlie laughs, and rips off the cover. He hands the box back to Norman, who squints at it.)*

ETHEL. What is it?

NORMAN. I still don't know.

ETHEL. Oh. It's your medicine.

NORMAN. Oh, goody. What a swell surprise.

ETHEL. Just in time. You'd nearly run out. *(To Charlie.)* It's nothing serious. Just for his palpitations.

NORMAN. Yes, Charlie, I have occasional heart throbs. *(Charlie laughs. Norman goes through the three or four envelopes.)* Look at this. A bill from Gas and Power in Wilmington, and we're not even there.

ETHEL. It's only a little bit each month.

NORMAN. *(Thrusting the letter at Charlie.)* Here, give this back to them. *(Ethel holds out her hand and Charlie passes it onto her.)* Since you're playing mailman, why don't you just deliver all of this to that old lady down there? *(He hands the other mail to Charlie, who laughs and passes it to Ethel.)* I've got to see what's happening in the world. I need some touch with reality. *(He unfolds the paper, Ethel looks through the envelopes.)*

ETHEL. Ah! A letter from Chelsea. *(She opens it eagerly.)*

CHARLIE. I noticed that. How is she? *(No one answers. Norman is studying the paper, Ethel digs into the long letter.)* Norman?

NORMAN. What?

CHARLIE. Chelsea.

NORMAN. Who?

CHARLIE. Your daughter, Chelsea.

NORMAN. What about her?

CHARLIE. How is she?

NORMAN. Oh. Forty-two.

CHARLIE. What? How *is* she?

NORMAN. Oh. I don't know. You'd have to ask her mother.

CHARLIE. Ethel?

ETHEL. Mmmm.

CHARLIE. How is she?

ETHEL. Mmm-mm.

CHARLIE. *(Turning back to Norman, who has opened the sports section.)* Is she really forty-two? Norman?

NORMAN. Who?

CHARLIE. Is Chelsea really forty-two?

NORMAN. That's what her mother says.

CHARLIE. Holy Mackinoly. And she went all the way through and never had kids, huh?

NORMAN. What? What do you mean, all the way through?

CHARLIE. Her childbearing years.

NORMAN. Oh. Yes. I suppose so.

CHARLIE. Hmmm.

ETHEL. She sounds as if she's having the best time.

CHARLIE. That's great.

NORMAN. Look at the goddam Red Sox.

CHARLIE. Where's she writing from? I couldn't make out the postmark.

NORMAN. What?

CHARLIE. Where's Chelsea writing from?

NORMAN. Home.

CHARLIE. I figured that. Where's she live now?

NORMAN. At home. Goddam Yankees.

ETHEL. *(Not looking up.)* On the coast.

CHARLIE. Oh.

NORMAN. Better tell him which coast, or he'll think she's living in Bar Harbor. It's California, Charlie.

CHARLIE. I knew that.

ETHEL. He knew that.

NORMAN. Goddam those Orioles. Baltimore has always been a sneaky town.

ETHEL. Oh, Norman, she says she's coming for your birthday. And she's bringing her friend. *(To Charlie.)* She has the nicest boyfriend.

CHARLIE. *(Not sounding thrilled.)* Oh.

NORMAN. She decided on her own to come, just like that? No prompting from anyone?

ETHEL. What? What are you saying?

NORMAN. Likely story. Mrs. Machiavelli.

ETHEL. They're coming together as part of a vacation, that's all, and then they're going on to Europe.

NORMAN. Ohhh. Well. I don't want crowds of people here on my birthday. I don't want crowds of people watching me turn older.

ETHEL. Oh, pooh. There'll just be the three of us. Is three a *crowd?*

NORMAN. That's what they say.

CHARLIE. That's right. Three's a crowd. *(He laughs. He stops, doing the math.)* What happened to her husband?

ETHEL. Wait a minute. It's not that Freddie person. This is a different boyfriend altogether.

NORMAN. What the hell is going on? Detroit has disappeared. It's gone completely. Good God!

ETHEL. What is it, Norman?

NORMAN. Detroit is gone. This stupid paper has them missing. *(To Charlie.)* Do you suppose they've been dropped from the league? *(Charlie shrugs.)* With that stupid commissioner, anything is possible.

CHARLIE. What happened to her husband?

ETHEL. *(Reading.)* Oh, my goodness.

NORMAN. *(Reading.)* What?

ETHEL. *(Looking up.)* What did you say, Charlie?

CHARLIE. I wondered what happened to Chelsea's husband.

ETHEL. He didn't work out.

NORMAN. He couldn't tell the difference between a Negro and an Italian.

CHARLIE. What?

NORMAN. The stupid commissioner. Talking about the so-called greats of the twentieth century, and he's got DiMaggio mixed up with Henry Aaron.

ETHEL. *(Reading.)* Oh, my goodness.

NORMAN. That's a pretty hard mistake to make. Good thing he wasn't in charge during the war. He would have invaded Newark in search of Mussolini. *(Charlie laughs.)* That wasn't a joke, Charlie. *(Charlie stops laughing.)*

ETHEL. She says she's in love. With a dentist.

NORMAN. Oh, really? Does her boyfriend know about this?

ETHEL. That is her boyfriend. Her new boyfriend is a dentist.

CHARLIE. That's interesting.

NORMAN. That's whom she's bringing here? A dentist?

ETHEL. Yes.

CHARLIE. Huh.

NORMAN. Oh, God. He'll be staring at our teeth all the time. Why does she have such a fascination with Jewish people?

25

ETHEL. Who said this one was Jewish?

NORMAN. He's a dentist, isn't he? Name me one dentist who isn't Jewish.

ETHEL. Your brother.

NORMAN. My brother is deceased. Name me one living dentist who isn't Jewish.

CHARLIE. Doctor Baylor.

NORMAN. Who is Doctor Baylor?

CHARLIE. My dentist.

NORMAN. He's in Maine, Charlie. There are no Jews in Maine.

CHARLIE. Sure there are. The Gittlemans over in Spruce Cove.

NORMAN. Those are tourists. Most tourists are Jewish.

CHARLIE. I know a Jewish guy who isn't a tourist. He runs a used car lot up in Augusta.

NORMAN. I'll bet he does. But, he's obviously an immigrant. From New York or somewhere. There are no native Jews in Maine. Just as there are no native Negroes here, or native Puerto Ricans.

ETHEL. I wouldn't think so.

NORMAN. I'm just pointing out to Charlie some of the charms of his habitat. Some of the reasons why we like it so well. *(To Charlie.)* We don't come here just for the bugs, you know. It's true you have your French Canadians, but at least they speak French. So, it's not quite as bad. Makes them sound intelligent.

ETHEL. *(To Norman.)* This particular dentist who's coming to celebrate your birthday is named Ray, and that doesn't sound Jewish.

NORMAN. It would depend on the last name, I'd say.

ETHEL. That is his last name.

NORMAN. His last name is Ray?

ETHEL. Yes. Bill Ray.

NORMAN. Bill Ray. That sounds rather flippant.

ETHEL. Well, shall we ask him not to come?

NORMAN. No. I think we should have representatives from all walks of life here for my last birthday party.

ETHEL. Oh, God. *(Then, to Charlie, brightly.)* I think this medicine should be put away from all this hot air. *(She carries it to the kitchen. Norman glowers after her, then turns his stare onto Charlie.)*

NORMAN. Why didn't you marry Chelsea?

CHARLIE. You wouldn't let me.

NORMAN. Oh. *(He thinks about it.)* You could have married someone else. I would have allowed that.

CHARLIE. I didn't want anyone else. I mean, I've come close. There's still time.

NORMAN. *(Going back to his paper.)* Oh, yes. You've got lots of time.

CHARLIE. How old will you be?

NORMAN. When?

CHARLIE. On your birthday.

NORMAN. One hundred and three.

CHARLIE. Really? *(He laughs.)* You're kidding. Miss Appley was ninety-seven in May. Isn't that amazing?

NORMAN. Yes. *(He turns to the classified ads.)*

CHARLIE. She died, you know.

NORMAN. No.

CHARLIE. Yup. Last Tuesday. We got a call. In case any mail came up.

NORMAN. They gave you a forwarding address for Miss Appley? *(Charlie laughs. Ethel comes back in.)*

ETHEL. Now what's going on here?

NORMAN. One of the lesbians expired. *(Charlie roars at this.)*

ETHEL. Oh, Norman. *(To Charlie.)* Which one?

CHARLIE. Miss Appley.

ETHEL. Oh, dear. Well, she had a good, full life.

NORMAN. Charlie says she was ninety-seven.

ETHEL. Really? How wonderful.

NORMAN. Puts us all to shame, doesn't it? There's something to be said for a deviant life style.

CHARLIE. I always liked those old ladies. But I sure used to wonder what the heck was going on in there. *(He winks at Norman, hoping for a response, but gets a disapproving look instead. Charlie stands, covering his embarrassment.)* Well, thanks for the coffee and the biscuits.

ETHEL. Any time, Charlie. You must come round when Chelsea's here.

CHARLIE. Oh, yuh. I haven't seen her for a long time. Must be ... well, let's see. It was the summer my father died, and I was thirty-six at the time. I'm forty-four now, so that's ... *(He figures in his head.)*

NORMAN. Eight years.

CHARLIE. Eight years. Holy Mackinoly. Well, see you tomorrow.

ETHEL. Okay, dear. *(They both look at Norman, who is engrossed in his paper.)* Norman, Charlie's leaving.

NORMAN. Good. *(He looks up.)* Bye!

CHARLIE. Goodbye, Norman.

NORMAN. Watch out for that screen door.

ETHEL. *(To Charlie.)* He really is a poop, isn't he? *(Charlie laughs, and exits out the big door and across the porch. Ethel closes the door and then calls to him.)* Seen our loons out there today?

CHARLIE. *(Offstage.)* Yup. Out by Honey Island. They're teaching their baby to fly.

ETHEL. Oh. How exciting. I hope they bring him over to introduce us. Bye, Charlie.

CHARLIE. *(Offstage.)* Bye!

ETHEL. Isn't that exciting? Teaching their baby to fly.

NORMAN. Listen to this: "Elderly gentleman wanted for companionship and conversation, for convalescing invalid. Three afternoons a week." Now, doesn't that sound perfect?

ETHEL. Perfect for you. I wouldn't have much hope for the invalid.

NORMAN. There's another one here: "Retired people sought for handbill delivery. Mornings or evenings. Some walking involved." I should call; I can walk.

ETHEL. Yes. I can just see you walking out there with those mosquitoes. You'd be eaten alive.

NORMAN. I could carry my screen door with me.

ETHEL. Is that why you came rushing back here? To read those silly ads?

NORMAN. Could be. Maybe I should have asked Charlie if he needs another man on the boat. I could balance out there on the deck, and do a belly flop at every dock we came to. Could be a source of amusement all around the lake. Be a great boon to the Postal Department. Get more people writing letters. What do you suppose Charlie would pay me?

ETHEL. Whatever is the matter with you? Why do you need a job? You've always loved being here on Golden Pond with nothing to do. Why is this summer any different?

NORMAN. I'm in the market for a last hurrah.

ETHEL. Lord. Why can't you just pick berries and catch fish and read books, and enjoy this sweet, sweet time?

NORMAN. *(After a pause.)* Do you want to know why I came back so fast with my little bucket? I got to the end of our lane, and I ... couldn't remember where the old town road was. I went a little way into the woods, and nothing looked familiar, not one tree.

And it scared me half to death. So I came running back here, to you, to see your pretty face, and to feel that I was safe. That I was still me. (*He puts his face in his hands. Ethel is stunned by his speech, but she rallies quickly. She bends over him and rubs his back.*)

ETHEL. Well, you're safe, you old poop. And you're definitely still you. Still picking on poor Charlie. After lunch, after we gobble up all the strawberries, I'll *take* you down to the old town road. You'll remember it all, my darling; we've walked it a thousand thousand times. And we'll pick us another batch of those little tiny berries. And I'll do the bending. You just talk away the mosquitoes. (*She rubs his back and smiles down at him sadly.*)

Scene 3

The middle of July. Early evening.

It is just the edge of darkness, there is still a soft glow in the sky. The room looks quite cheery. A large poster hangs on the stage right wall. It reads: Happy Birthday Norman. There are several balloons flung about. As the scene progresses and it grows darker outside, little lights may be visible in the distance, other cottages.

After a moment, Ethel enters from the kitchen, carrying another poster. She wears jeans again, and a sweater now. She looks about for a place to put the sign. She crosses to the mantel and props it against the chimney. It says: Welcome Home, Chelsea. She looks at it, pleased. She looks about the room. Suddenly she rushes up to the porch door, which is open, the screen back in place. She speaks to the door.

ETHEL. Get away, you nasty things. Tsk. (*She waves her hands.*) Get off the door! (*She slaps the screen door.*) Get off, go on! (*She slaps the door harder. It falls over and onto the porch.*) Oh, Norman, for God's sake! (*She screams quietly.*) Acch! Get away, get away! (*She quickly closes the big door, and leans against it.*) Worse this year than ever. (*She cranks closed one of the windows. Norman appears on the stairs. He is dressed quite nattily in slacks and a shirt, a bright "scenic" tie, and a cardigan sweater. He pauses on the landing.)*

NORMAN. Whatever is going on down here?

ETHEL. You and your screen door. The *moths* are trying to get in. I swear you're on their side.

NORMAN. They're just trying to crash my party. It's expected to be the social highlight of the summer season, you know.

ETHEL. My, my, look at you. You have on a tie.

NORMAN. Yes, I know. I put it there. Do you think I've over-dressed?

ETHEL. I think I'm going to have to do some mighty fast maneuvers to catch up with you.

NORMAN. I have other ties. You could come as Miss Appley.

ETHEL. Thank you.

NORMAN. *(Looking at his sign.)* You've really outdone yourself with all this. *(He looks to the fireplace.)* "Welcome home, Chelsea." I see my birthday wasn't cause enough for a celebration.

ETHEL. Tsk. I just want our little girl to feel welcome.

NORMAN. Ah. Did you know our little girl has passed through her childbearing years without bearing any children?

ETHEL. Of course I know that. She chose not to, is all.

NORMAN. Hmmm. Seems odd, doesn't it? *(He comes down the steps.)* Did you ever have that woman-to-woman chat with her you said you were going to? Maybe she didn't know how.

ETHEL. Yes, I told her how. Twenty-five years ago. She seemed to know what I was talking about .

NORMAN. Maybe I should have taken that husband of hers aside. He could have used a few tips. I've never known anyone so timid in my life.

ETHEL. Every poor soul she's brought home has been timid around you . You attack them so.

NORMAN. I don't, you know.

ETHEL. *(Pointedly.)* Wouldn't it be nice if we could all get along this time?

NORMAN. Oh, sure.

ETHEL. I wonder whom I could talk to to arrange that sort of thing.

NORMAN. I intend to be the perfect host. I'll overwhelm them with my charm.

ETHEL. Mm-hmm. That's what I'm afraid of.

NORMAN. *(He looks about.)* Well…Why aren't they here? I'm getting older by the minute.

ETHEL. They said they'll be here when they get here.

NORMAN. Is that what they said? That's a hell of an attitude. No wonder we have no grandchildren.

ETHEL. What would we do with grandchildren?

NORMAN. Toss them on our knees. We're the last of the Thayers, you know. End of the line for a damn good name.

ETHEL. Well, we'll take it out in style. Shhh. *(From the lake can be heard the plaintive call of the loon.)* Norman, the loons. *(The call is repeated. She peers out the window.)* They're calling. Oh, why is it so dark?

NORMAN. Because the sun went down.

ETHEL. I wish I could see them. *(She calls.)* Yoo hoo! Loooooooons! *(Norman stares at her.)* Loony looo-oooons!

NORMAN. I don't think you should do that in front of Chelsea's companion.

ETHEL. Oh, pooh. I'm just talking to my friends. *(She calls again.)* Yoo hooo! *(Now there is the sound of a car in the back of the house.)* Oh, no! They're here! And I'm not dressed!

NORMAN. You look dressed.

ETHEL. Oh, no, I wanted to look nice. I look like an old character.

NORMAN. You *are* an old character. Run upstairs and change. I'll stay here and entertain them. I'll make them feel welcome.

ETHEL. Will you be nice to them?

NORMAN. Sure. I'll explain to them the risk involved in arriving late for an old man's birthday party. *(The door opens and Chelsea Thayer Wayne steps in. Pretty if perhaps the tiniest bit heavy, athletic and tan but with a nervous edginess to her, and plenty of her father's humor. She rushes to Ethel.)*

CHELSEA. Mommy. *(They embrace. Quite intensely. She looks to Norman, who hasn't moved.)* Hello, Norman.

NORMAN. Look at you.

CHELSEA. Happy birthday.

NORMAN. *(Fending off any emotion he may be feeling.)* Look at this little fat girl, Ethel.

ETHEL. Oh stop, she's as thin as a rail. Isn't she, Norman?

NORMAN. Yes. *(There follows a moment of adjustment. Nothing is said. Ethel jumps in quickly.)*

ETHEL. Dear Chelsea. I'm so glad you're home.

CHELSEA. Oh, God. I thought we'd never get here. We rented a car that explodes every forty miles.

NORMAN. You rented a car?

CHELSEA. Yes, in Boston.

NORMAN. Huh. What sort of car is it?

CHELSEA. Oh, I don't know. Red, I think.

ETHEL. *(Very cheerily.)* Ooh! A red car!

NORMAN. No, I meant — what sort of make is it?

CHELSEA. *(Stymied.)* Um. I don't know.

ETHEL. She doesn't know, dear. It doesn't matter.

NORMAN. Of course it doesn't matter. I was just curious.

CHELSEA. Well, I should have looked, I guess. It's um, very ugly and it breaks down a lot.

NORMAN. Ugly and it breaks down a lot. That sounds like a [Nash]. I bet they bought up all the old [Nashes] all over the country and are renting them to unsuspecting customers.

CHELSEA. I'll bet.

NORMAN. I'll bet, too.

CHELSEA. Well. Okay. *(A standoff. She turns away.)* Well. The old house looks exactly the same.

NORMAN. The old house *is* exactly the same. Just older. Like its inhabitants.

CHELSEA. Well …

ETHEL. Where's your friend? You did bring your friend, didn't you?

CHELSEA. I knew I was forgetting something.

NORMAN. That's still on then, huh?

CHELSEA. As far as I know. It was two minutes ago. I may have been deserted. It wouldn't be the first time. Are you two ready?

ETHEL. Of course. We can't wait.

NORMAN. That's right. We can't wait.

CHELSEA. Great. *(She steps toward the door and calls.)* Hey! Come on in. Nobody's going to bite you. I hope. *(Norman and Ethel watch expectantly and Billy Ray enters. He is thirteen, short and flippant, but only to cover his awkwardness. He is eager and bright, his hair long, his posture terrible. He carries a backpack, a duffel bag and a boom box into the room, dumping them unceremoniously on the floor, as Norman and Ethel watch in wonder.)* Mommy and Norman, this is Billy Ray.

BILLY. How ya doin'?

NORMAN. You seem awfully young to be a dentist.

BILLY. I'm a midget.

NORMAN. Oh, really?

CHELSEA. This is Billy Ray, Junior.

NORMAN. Oh. I'm Norman Thayer, Junior.

CHELSEA. His dad is out trying to soothe the car.

ETHEL. *(Stepping forward.)* What a nice surprise! Hello, Billy.

You can call me Ethel. And you can call Norman Norman.

CHELSEA. I like your logic, Mommy. *(She steps to the door.)* I better see if Bill's gotten lost. He was trying to turn around. He probably drove into the lake. *(She exits. Ethel steps to the door and looks out. Norman and Billy stare at each other.)*

ETHEL. It's so dark outside. It never used to be this dark.

BILLY. I hear you turned eighty today.

NORMAN. Is that what you heard?

BILLY. Yeah. That's really old.

NORMAN. Oh? You should meet my father.

BILLY. Your father's still alive?

NORMAN. No. But you should meet him.

ETHEL. *(Turning back to the room.)* This is so much fun! Norman, why don't we put Billy in Chelsea's old room and then he can look out on the lake in the morning.

NORMAN. Why don't we put him out on the float and he can look at the lake all night long.

BILLY. I'd like that.

ETHEL. I'm afraid you'd be eaten alive by all the bugs.

NORMAN. So?

ETHEL. Norman, take him up and show him where everything is.

NORMAN. Come on, boy. Get your clutter. *(Billy does and he follows Norman up the stairs.)*

BILLY. I just had a birthday, too. I turned thirteen two weeks ago.

NORMAN. We're practically twins.

BILLY. We're sixty-six years and fifty weeks apart.

NORMAN. You're quick, aren't you?

BILLY. Oh, yeah. *(They go into the room at the landing. Chelsea steps back in downstairs.)*

CHELSEA. He's coming. He thought he had to lock the doors.

ETHEL. Well, you never know; the changes around here.

CHELSEA. *(Stepping to Ethel.)* Norman looks very old.

ETHEL. Really? Well, I don't know.

CHELSEA. You look great though.

ETHEL. Thank you. So do you. I love your hair like that.

CHELSEA. You do? *(She touches her hair self-consciously. She leans to her mother, not noticing Norman appear on the landing above.)* How's his mind? Is he remembering things any better?

ETHEL. Oh, he's all right.

NORMAN. (*Loudly.*) Come on, Billy. I'll show you the bathroom, if I can remember where it is. *(He disappears into the hallway. Bill*

Ray bursts through the door. Attractive and well-dressed, a tad self-serious but with a good sense of humor when he remembers to use it. He drops his several suitcases, out of breath and more than a little rattled.)

CHELSEA. Look at you. You made it.

BILL. Yes. I think I saw a bear.

CHELSEA. I doubt that. Bill, this is my mother. Mommy, Bill Ray.

ETHEL. *(Shaking Bill's hand.)* I'm very pleased you could come. Welcome to Golden pond.

BILL. Thank you. Do you have a dog?

ETHEL. What? No. *(To Chelsea.)* You know, I tried to interest Norman in getting a dog this summer, but he went into some morbid diatribe about how unfair it is to take on a puppy if you're planning to die soon.

CHELSEA. You could have gotten him an old dog. Something on its last leg.

ETHEL. Well, Norman is still in mourning for Chum, I'm afraid.

CHELSEA. *(To Bill.)* Chum was a Labrador retriever who passed on just twenty short years ago.

BILL. *(Not exactly following.)* Oh. Do any of your neighbors have dogs?

ETHEL. Um. No, I don't believe so.

BILL. Then I definitely saw a bear.

ETHEL. Oh, no, I don't think there'd be a bear out there this time of year. They go pretty far into the woods when the summer people show up. There are a lot of very nasty moths flying around, though, I'm sorry to say.

BILL. This was kind of big for a moth.

CHELSEA. Probably a wild boar, then. *(Bill looks at her, not immediately comforted by her Norman-like drollery. She smiles, taking his hand.)* Bill, you want to visit the men's room before you go through the shock of meeting my father?

BILL. Huh? Uh. No. I'm all right. *(There is a clatter on the stairs, and Billy leaps down, followed by Norman.)*

CHELSEA. Too late anyway.

BILLY. Dad. They do have indoor plumbing.

BILL. *(Embarrassed.)* Oh. Good.

BILLY. *(Crossing down into the room.)* Chelsea was bullshitting us.

BILL. Billy.

CHELSEA. *(To Ethel.)* I always try to paint a rustic picture of life on Golden Pond.

ETHEL. Oh, it's rustic all right.

BILL. It's lovely, though. Lovely rusticity. *(He turns warily, feeling Norman bearing down on him.)*

NORMAN. We've been peeing indoors for forty years.

BILL. Oh. You must be Norman.

NORMAN. Yes, I must be. Who are you?

BILL. Bill Ray. *(He puts out his hand. Norman shakes it.)*

NORMAN. Bill Ray. The dentist?

BILL. Um. Yes.

NORMAN. Want to see my teeth? *(He bares them.)*

ETHEL. Norman.

BILL. *(Smiling.)* I just want to tell you how glad I am to be here, sir. Chelsea talks so much about you and your wife and your wonderful house on the lake, and I'm very pleased that she's brought us here.

NORMAN. *(He stares at Bill a moment, then turns to Chelsea.)* Charlie's been asking for you.

CHELSEA. Charlie? *(Norman responds by mimicking Charlie's laugh.)* Holy Mackinoly. *(To Bill.)* Charlie is our mailman. He was also my boyfriend every summer for twelve years. He taught me everything.

BILL. *(Goodnaturedly.)* Isn't that amazing?

NORMAN. It is when you know Charlie. *(A pause.)*

CHELSEA. Well. I'm going to say hello to the lake. Anyone like to come?

BILLY. Me. I've never seen anyone say hello to a lake.

CHELSEA. Then this will be a valuable experience for you, wise guy. It's always my first order of business when I get to Golden Pond. Coming, Mommy?

ETHEL. Yes! Want to take the boat?

BILLY. Yeah!

CHELSEA. Why not? Let's go, Bill.

BILL. Where? Outside?

CHELSEA. That's where the lake is. *(She heads for the door. Ethel and Billy follow.)* Coming, Norman?

NORMAN. Nope.

ETHEL. Oh, come on.

NORMAN. No. I'm just going to sit here and enjoy the quiet.

CHELSEA. Oh. Um … *(She looks to Ethel, and then at Bill.)*

BILL. I think I'll stay, too.

ETHEL. Come on, Norman.

NORMAN. Don't be silly. I want to sit here and enjoy the quiet. With Bill. We can talk baseball.

BILL. Great.

35

CHELSEA. Great.

ETHEL. I'll get the yard light. *(She reaches by the door and flicks it. The trees light up.)* I generally keep it off to discourage the June bugs. *(She starts to open the door.)* Now, we're going to have to make a run for it all at once. Ready? *(She opens the door and pushes Billy through. Chelsea follows.)*

CHELSEA. The screen door has fallen down.

ETHEL. Oh, really? Norman will fix it. *(She steps through the door, closing it. Their voices can be heard as they cross the porch and disappear down the steps. Norman, in the meantime, has sat down in his chair. Bill stands for a moment, a shade uncomfortable.)*

BILL. So. You're a baseball fan, huh?

NORMAN. No.

BILL. Oh. I like baseball. I like the Dodgers.

NORMAN. Oh, really? They moved out west somewhere, didn't they?

BILL. Um. Yes. To Los Angeles. Some years ago.

NORMAN. They still in the big leagues?

BILL. Oh, yes. They're a real powerhouse in the National League West.

NORMAN. Well, bless their little hearts. *(There is a long pause.)*

BILL. Um. How does it feel to turn eighty?

NORMAN. It feels twice as bad as it did turning forty.

BILL. Oh, well, I know what that's like.

NORMAN. Do you?

BILL. Yes. I turned forty five years ago. I'm forty-five now. *(Realizing how stupid that sounded, he forges on.)* I … love your house.

NORMAN. It's not for sale.

BILL. Oh, no. I wasn't thinking about buying it. I just like it.

NORMAN. Oh. Me, too.

BILL. It has a charming ambiance.

NORMAN. Does it?

BILL. Yes. Norman?

NORMAN. Yes?

BILL. May I call you Norman?

NORMAN. I believe you just did.

BILL. I don't want to press.

NORMAN. No.

BILL. I'll call you Norman then.

NORMAN. Fine.

BILL. What shall I call your wife?

NORMAN. How about Ethel? That's her name. Ethel Thayer. Thoundth ath ith I'm lithping, doethn't it? Ethel Thayer. It almost kept her from marrying me. She wanted me to change my last name to hers.

BILL. What was that?

NORMAN. I don't remember. Ethel's all you need to know. That's the name she goes by.

BILL. I never knew. Chelsea always calls her Mommy.

NORMAN. There's a reason for that.

BILL. But she calls you Norman.

NORMAN. There's a reason for that, too. *(He pauses.)* I *am* her father, if you're trying to figure it out. I'm her father but not her daddy. Ethel is her mommy, and I'm Norman.

BILL. *(Confused.)* Oh. Is it all right if I sit down?

NORMAN. As far as I'm concerned it is. *(Bill sits. Norman stares at him. Bill tries to smile. Norman abruptly rises.)* I think I'll start a new book. See if I can finish it before I'm finished myself. Maybe a novelette. *(He steps to the shelves and studies the collection.)* Maybe something in Reader's Digest Condensed. *(He pulls down a book.)* Here's *Swiss Family Robinson.* Ever read it?

BILL. Oh, yes. It's great. I'd recommend it.

NORMAN. No need for that. I've read it, too. *(He sits again.)* But my mind's going so it'll all be new to me. *(He opens the book.)* Has that son of yours read this book?

BILL. I … don't think so.

NORMAN. Your son hasn't read *Swiss Family Robinson?*

BILL. No. But I intend to have him read it. I'm afraid his mother's been the motivating force in his life the last few years, the poor kid, and now I'm making a move to eradicate some of the … dishevelment. *(Norman stares at Bill without comment. He returns to his book. Bill feels compelled to communicate.)* Yeah, things are coming together for me pretty nicely now. The practice is real strong, and I'm feeling very good about myself. Meeting Chelsea has been a major…thing. And she's really flowering. She likes her job a lot, and she's been doing some beautiful paintings. We have a very kinetic relationship. Very positive. I'm sure you'd be pleased. *(Norman looks up. There is a pause.)*

NORMAN. What do you charge for a filling?

BILL. Huh?

NORMAN. You're a dentist, aren't you? What do you charge for a filling?

BILL. Um. Start at about [ninety-five dollars].

NORMAN. [Ninety-five dollars]?! Good God! My brother charged [fifteen dollars] a filling right up until [1988] when he raised it to [twenty]. That's when I stopped going to him.

BILL. Your brother is a dentist?

NORMAN. He was. When he was living.

BILL. Isn't that amazing?

NORMAN. I don't know. I think every family has one. *(He returns to his book. Bill studies him, then chooses his words with care.)*

BILL. Norman. Um. I don't want to offend you, but there's a rather important little topic that I feel I have to broach.

NORMAN. *(Looking up.)* I beg your pardon?

BILL. I don't want to offend you, but ... if it's all right with you, we'd like to sleep together.

NORMAN. What do you mean?

BILL. We'd like to sleep ... together ... in the same room ... in the same bed. If you don't find that offensive.

NORMAN. All three of you?

BILL. What? Oh, no. Just two.

NORMAN. You and Billy?

BILL. No.

NORMAN. Not Chelsea and Billy?

BILL. No, sir.

NORMAN. That leaves only Chelsea and you then.

BILL. Yes.

NORMAN. Why would I find that offensive? You're not planning on doing something unusual, are you?

BILL. Oh, no. Just ... *(He can't go on.)*

NORMAN. That doesn't seem too offensive, as long as you're quiet.

BILL. Great.

NORMAN. Chelsea always used to sleep in the same bed with her husband.

BILL. Oh, I'm sure.

NORMAN. And Ethel and I do, you know. We sleep together. Been doing it for years.

BILL. Well, of course. But you're married and all.

NORMAN. So?

BILL. Well ...

NORMAN. I think I'm beginning to see this more clearly. It's a moral issue, isn't it?

38

BILL. Well, it's just that we're of different generations, different mores …

NORMAN. What is a more? I've never known.

BILL. Um … a custom, I'd say. Or something.

NORMAN. Go on. Forgive me for interrupting.

BILL. Well, it's just a matter of points of view …

NORMAN. *(Interrupting.)* I shouldn't have interrupted.

BILL. Oh. Of course. *(Starting again.)* It's just that I don't want our relationship to …

NORMAN. It's a terrible social problem, I think.

BILL. Um…?

NORMAN. Interrupting. Not listening. The art of conversation went out with radio probably.

BILL. Yes.

NORMAN. Or maybe with mirrors.

BILL. Um …

NORMAN. Ever notice how people start to check themselves out in a mirror or a window or your eyeglasses when they're supposed to be listening?

BILL. Yes, I have noticed that.

NORMAN. It's a shifty sort of quality, I think.

BILL. Yes.

NORMAN. Or perhaps it's just a form of egocentricity.

BILL. Yeah.

NORMAN. I do it.

BILL. You do?

NORMAN. Sure. Conversations bore me to tears. I always look for a little divertissement while I'm waiting for my turn to talk.

BILL. Huh.

NORMAN. Pretty shabby, huh?

BILL. Well …

NORMAN. I don't do it with Ethel. She's so pretty, isn't she?

BILL. Yes.

NORMAN. After all these years I still can't get over how pretty she is. Or how handsome I am. That's the real reason I always look for a mirror. I like to keep checking. Make sure I haven't faded.

BILL. Oh.

NORMAN. They say you fade with old age. They say your looks just go. Haven't seen a sign of it.

BILL. No, indeed.

NORMAN. What were we talking about?

BILL. Um …

NORMAN. Sex, I believe. You were concerned that my morals somehow wouldn't mesh with yours.

BILL. Yes.

NORMAN. Don't be silly. I'd be delighted to have you abusing my daughter under my own roof.

BILL. Um …

NORMAN. Would you like the room where I first violated her mother, or would you be interested in the master bedroom?

BILL. Norman …

NORMAN. Ethel and your son and I could all sleep out back and you could do it right here on the hearth. Like that idea?

BILL. *(He's embarrassed, but he's also heard enough. He smiles at Norman and shakes his head.)* You're having a good time, aren't you?

NORMAN. Hmmm?

BILL. Chelsea told me all about you, about how you like to have a good time with people's heads. She does it, too, sometimes, and sometimes I can get into it. Sometimes not. I just want you to know that I'm very good at recognizing crap when I hear it. You know, it's not imperative that you and I be friends, but it might be *nice.* I'm sure you're a fascinating person, and I'm sure it would be fascinating to get to know you. That's obviously not an easy task. But it's all right, you go ahead and be has *poopy* as you want, to quote Chelsea, and I'll be as receptive and as pleasant as I can. I just want you to bear in mind while we're sitting here smiling at each other and you're jerking me around that I know precisely what you're up to and that I can take only so much of it. Okay? Good. *(He pauses. Waits for a reaction. Norman has been listening very intently.)* Now. What's the bottom line on the illicit sex question?

NORMAN. *(He stares at Bill for a long moment, then smiles.)* Very nice. Good speech. I liked that a lot. So, bottom line, huh? You're a bottom-line man. All right. Here's the bottom line: oh-kay. Ethel and I haven't always been married. It just seems that way. We tipped over a canoe or two in our day, trying to accommodate another generation's *mores. (He pauses.)* You seem like a nice person, a bit verbose perhaps, a bit outspoken, but … nice.

BILL. Thank you.

NORMAN. And you're right about me. I *am* fascinating.

BILL. I'm sure you are.

NORMAN. I didn't mean to weight down our conversation. We can go back to talking about sex if you like.

BILL. Oh, no. That's okay.

NORMAN. I like talking about sex. Anything you want to know, just ask me.

BILL. Okay. I ... I do want to make sure I have this little matter clear in my mind. Chelsea and I *can* sleep together, right?

NORMAN. Yes! Please do! Just don't let Ethel catch you. *(There is the sound of footsteps on the porch steps, and Billy comes bounding in the door.)*

BILLY. Dad! I paddled a canoe! It's a boat, just like the Indians had! *(Bill stands.)*

NORMAN. Actually the Indians used a different grade of aluminum.

BILLY. Chelsea wants you to come down, Dad. She and Ethel are going skinny-dipping.

BILL. Skinny-dipping? *(He barely looks at Norman.)* Um ...

NORMAN. Go ahead. Permissiveness runs rampant up here on Golden Pond. *(Bill walks slowly to the front door. He turns.)*

BILL. Are there ever any bears around these parts?

NORMAN. Oh, sure. Black bears and grizzlies. One came along here last month and ate an old lesbian.

BILL. Uh ...

BILLY. Go on, Dad. He's bullshitting you.

BILL. Heh. *(He nods. Takes a deep breath and steps bravely out.)* God, I hope I live through the next few days. *(He exits. Norman watches Billy explore the room, picking up whatever makes him curious.)*

NORMAN. You like that word, don't you? Bullshit.

BILLY. Yeah.

NORMAN. It's a good word.

BILLY. You going skinny-dipping?

NORMAN. Nope. You?

BILLY. Naw. I try to be selective about who I flash in front of.

NORMAN. *(Not following.)* Oh?

BILLY. Chelsea says you're a real heavy-duty fisherman. She calls you The Old Man of the Sea.

NORMAN. Ah. I've caught a few. You fish?

BILLY. No.

NORMAN. Want to go sometime?

BILLY. Maybe.

NORMAN. All right. We'll see. What do you think of your father?

BILLY. To tell you the truth, he's not bad.

NORMAN. *(Watching him critically.)* Why do you walk with your

41

shoulders all bent like that?

BILLY. I have a lot on my mind.

NORMAN. Oh. *(He studies Billy for a moment.)* Well, what do you do out there in California, since you don't fish? I mean, what does one do for recreation, when one is thirteen and not in school?

BILLY. Cruise chicks.

NORMAN. Um…?

BILLY. Meet'em. Girls. Try to pick them up.

NORMAN. Oh. And what do you do with them when you have them?

BILLY. Suck face.

NORMAN. I beg your pardon?

BILLY. *(Explaining.)* You know. Kiss. Suck face — kiss.

NORMAN. Oh. *(He stares at Billy, then looks at the book he still holds.)* Ever read this book? *Swiss Family Robinson?*

BILLY. No.

NORMAN. Go read it.

BILLY. Now?

NORMAN. Yes. Go upstairs and read the first chapter. And give me a report tomorrow. *(He hands Billy the book.)* Go on.

BILLY. Well, I thought we were going to have a party.

NORMAN. I'll call you when the party's underway, if it ever is. Go on. Read the first chapter. You'll like it. *(Billy obeys. There's something in Norman's authority that Billy responds to, not unfavorably. He marches up the stairs.)* Let me see you stand up straight. *(Billy stops and scowls at Norman.)* Come on. Nobody has that much on his mind. *(Billy straightens.)* Ah! Very good! You should try that more often. It will make it easier to bear your heavy load.

NORMAN. *(Billy exits. Ethel comes bursting in the upstage door, fully dressed, and swatting at the moths.)* I thought you'd be nude.

ETHEL. Sorry. The water feels lovely, but I didn't want to overwhelm Chelsea's friend on his first night here. *(She comes down into the room.)* Have you been picking on him?

NORMAN. Yes. He found me fascinating. He said they want to sleep together.

ETHEL. I expected that. Well. Why not? They're big people.

NORMAN. Yes.

ETHEL. You and I did it. Didn't we?

NORMAN. Yes, I told him that.

ETHEL. *(Blushes.)* Well, you didn't have to tell him. I think I better get us some dinner together. You must be starved half to death.

NORMAN. And then some.

ETHEL. *(Heading for the kitchen.)* Where's the boy?

NORMAN. I sent him to his room with a good book.

ETHEL. Oh. *(She looks up toward the landing.)* Well. *(She starts into the kitchen, stops, comes back to Norman.)* Norman.

NORMAN. Yes.

ETHEL. Norman. There's something I want us to do for Chelsea: Let her leave Billy with us for a month.

NORMAN. Which Billy?

ETHEL. The little one. *Billy.* Bill is supposed to have him for the summer, and he'd be miserable in Europe. They could pick him up in August. And they could be alone. Bill seems very nice, and Chelsea needs someone nice. Couldn't we do that for her?

NORMAN. What would we do with the boy? What would I say to him?

ETHEL. You'd think of something. Norman, let's do it. Let's say we'll do it, and give Chelsea some happiness. Yes?

NORMAN. *(After the briefest pause.)* All right.

ETHEL. *(Hugging him.)* You poop. I love you. We're going to have a splendid time, the three of us. You really are the sweetest man in the world. And I'm the only one who knows. I've *got* to make some dinner. *(She heads for the kitchen.)* Can you hold out ten minutes?

NORMAN. No. I'm going to bed.

ETHEL. *(Stopping.)* Oh, you're not.

NORMAN. No. I'm not. I was just bullshitting you. *(She shakes her head, continuing into the kitchen as Norman follows.)*

End of Act One

ACT TWO

Scene 1

The middle of August. Early morning. Outside, the sky is gray. After a moment Norman enters from the kitchen with a tackle box. He stands at the bottom of the stairs and calls, softly.

NORMAN. Billy, are you up? Let's go. Don't wake up the old lady. *(He crosses back to the rack and picks up two fishing poles, then gently pushes open the screen door, which is, remarkably enough, fastened on. He closes it carefully and disappears down the porch steps. No sooner has he gone than Billy enters downstage right carrying a bait can. He sets the bait can on the newel post and exits to the kitchen. Ethel appears at the top of the stairs, dressed in a well-traveled robe. Her attention is focused on a beam above her. She makes a face at it, and then crosses purposefully to the downstage right door and exits. Norman enters upstage right. Sees the bait can and stares at it, puzzled. He steps to the landing and picks it up.)* Billy! Let's go, boy. I've got the bait can. Don't wake up Ethel! *(He exits upstage with the bait can. Billy enters from the kitchen with a paper bag full of cookies, eating one as he goes. Until he trips on the rug and stumbles, the cookies spilling under the coffee table.)*

BILLY. *(Quietly, sounding like Norman.)* Good God! *(He grabs the bag and kneels quickly behind the couch, out of sight. Ethel enters downstage carrying a long leaf rake. She stands beneath the beam and stares up at it. She raises the rake high over her head and concentrates on the beam. Norman enters, his vision so blocked by the boat cushions he's carrying, the fishnet, the tackle box, the umbrella, the coil of rope and the bait can that he doesn't see Ethel. He steps to the bottom of the stairs and calls, a little less softly.)*

NORMAN. Let's go! *(Ethel hasn't particularly noticed him, her concentration on the beam being so intense. Now she's found her foe and she swings her rake mightily. It misses the beam altogether, and smacks down on the floor beside Norman. He is more than a little surprised.*

44

He drops his collection. Billy's head pops up, he looks, then goes back out of sight.) Good God! You must be mad! You're trying to kill me! *(He's not bothering with any quiet now.)*

ETHEL. That's not true. I was trying to kill a daddy-longlegs, but he got away.

NORMAN. You shouldn't be allowed to carry a dangerous weapon like this.

ETHEL. There's no need for you to go on shouting. You'll wake the boy.

NORMAN. *(Shouting.)* Good! I've been trying to wake him for twenty minutes. We're going fishing.

ETHEL. Oh, let him sleep. You drag him out every day, the poor thing. We have enough fish now as it is. What are we going to do with them all?

NORMAN. Feed them to the daddy-longlegs. *(He calls.)* You! Billy! Get it in gear, boy!

ETHEL. Let him sleep. It's going to rain anyway. The loons were calling for it all night long.

NORMAN. I didn't hear them. *(Suddenly there comes the sound of a loon calling. Norman and Ethel look at each other.)*

NORMAN. Well? What's the weather forecast now?

ETHEL. Still rain. *(The call is repeated.)* Isn't it lovely? What a sweet song they sing. *(Again the call.)* They must be right out in front.

NORMAN. Sounds to me as if they're right in this room. Out, boy! *(Billy rises from behind the couch, grinning from ear to ear. He calls again.)*

ETHEL. We have a joker here.

BILLY. Good morning, loonies.

ETHEL. Oh, yes, very funny.

BILLY. Let's get it in gear, Norman.

NORMAN. Watch it. *(Ethel watches as Billy comes around with his bag of cookies. He bends to pick up some of what Norman has dropped.)*

ETHEL. You two will be sorry when it begins to pour.

NORMAN. It's a chance we have to take. Billy still has to catch one more biggie. It's starting to depress him that I've outbiggied him.

BILLY. Today's the day. I can feel it.

ETHEL. What's in the bag, Billy?

BILLY. This bag? Food. Good food.

ETHEL. Not my Toll House cookies by any chance?

BILLY. Uh. Some.

ETHEL. *(Stepping to him.)* Hand it over. *(He does, reluctantly. Ethel takes the bag into the kitchen.)*

NORMAN. Spoilsport. *(To Billy.)* Oh, well. We can always eat raw fish the way the Orientals do.

BILLY. Blecch.

NORMAN. Of course you may never get any taller. Got a book with you?

BILLY. Yes. *(He doesn't, but he crosses quickly to the shelves and pulls down a book.)* A Connecticut Yankee in King Arthur's Court.

NORMAN. Ah. *(Ethel returns with a different bag, a larger canvas one, full to the top. She hangs it around Billy's neck.)*

ETHEL. You'll find a few cookies in there, and some biscuits, along with two tuna-fish sandwiches each, a thermos of milk, and a nice jar of fresh raspberries, just picked.

BILLY. Smooth move.

NORMAN. Right on, cool breeze. That's jive talk, Ethel.

ETHEL. That's nice. *(The boys head for the upstage door.)*

NORMAN. Goodbye, woman. Hold it! Where's my chair? I can't fish without my chair.

BILLY. It's in the back by the picnic table.

NORMAN. What's it doing there?

BILLY. You were sitting on it yesterday while you watched me clean the fish.

NORMAN. Ohhh.

ETHEL. Tsk. Has he been making you clean those stupid fish?

BILLY. Yeah.

NORMAN. That's right, Ethel. He cleans the stupid ones and I clean the smart ones. Fortunately the smarts ones are too smart to get caught. That's why they're in schools, ha ha!

ETHEL. Oh, Lord.

BILLY. *(To Norman.)* You're really becoming a nitwit, aren't you?

NORMAN. A *nitwit?* Hear that, Ethel? This poor child is starting to talk like an old lady. Get my chair, boy!

ETHEL. Norman, his hands are full.

BILLY. That's right, my hands are full.

NORMAN. So? You've got teeth, don't you?

ETHEL. Norman, *get* the chair.

NORMAN. Good God!

ETHEL. Poor Billy ends up doing all your chores.

NORMAN. What's the point of having a dwarf if he doesn't do chores? *(He kisses Ethel with great flair and exits. She shakes her head, exasperated but secretly pleased. She piles the gear back onto Billy.)*

46

BILLY. You could come with us, you know.

ETHEL. No, thank you, I've never liked fishing. I used to go with my father and brother. It always seemed as if the dead fish were staring at me.

BILLY. I know what you mean. But I like fishing.

ETHEL. I'm awfully glad. I know Norman loves having you go.

BILLY. Oh, yeah, we have a lot of fun. We don't just fish, you know.

ETHEL. No?

BILLY. Nope. We make good use of our time. Norman makes me practice my French, and I make him tell me stories from the old days. Sometimes he calls me Chelsea.

ETHEL. Oh. Well, you probably remind him of her in some ways.

BILLY. Yeah. I always say, "Norman, you know I'm not Chelsea; I'm Billy

NORMAN. *(Offstage.)* Hey! Allons! Debut!

BILLY. *(Calling.)* Je viens! *(To Ethel.)* That mean's I'm coming.

ETHEL. I'll get la porte.

BILLY. I wouldn't worry about Norman. I'll keep an eye on him.

ETHEL. Thank you. *(She holds the door as he lugs out the fishing gear. He gives her a final lusty salute.)*

BILLY. Goodbye, woman! *(He exits. She watches him go. She closes the screen door. She turns back to the room. Stops for a beat. Her attention is caught by a daddy-longlegs on the mantel. She grabs a newspaper and pursues the bug.)*

ETHEL. All right, hold it right there! Stay still! What's the matter with you? Look out, Elmer, he's right behind you! Oh, fiddle. Go on, climb the chimney, I don't care. Are you laughing at me? *(She takes down Elmer and hugs him to her.)* Oh, Elmer. *(She stands for a moment, lost in thought. The sound of the boat horn interrupts her. She turns and walks to the downstage right porch. She waves. She takes Elmer's hand and waves it. She sits on the railing.)* They say the lake is dying, but I don't believe it. They say all those houses along Koochakiyi Shores are killing Golden Pond. See, Elmer: no more yellow tents in the trees, no more bell calling the girls to supper. I left you in the window, Elmer, sitting on the sill, so you could look out at Camp Koochakiyi, when I was eight and nine and ten. And I'd stand on the bank, across the cove, at sunset, and I'd wave. And you always waved back, didn't you, Elmer? *(She thinks for a moment and then sings softly.)*

    I can see the birds,

    Way up in the sky,

From my tent on the bank of the lake
At Camp Koochakiyi
Koochakiyi

(She stops and considers it.) What a terrible song. *(But she sings on, tentatively adding a few long-forgotten dance steps.)*

We are the girls from Camp Koochakiyi
You can tell who we are by the gleam
In our eyes.
Our minds are clear and our hearts
Are strong.
We are dancing here, but we won't be long.
There will soon be deer where there now
Are fawns.
But we'll remember our years on Golden Pond.
On Golden Pond.

(Near the end of the performance, Chelsea steps into the house. She listens, touched. She steps out to her mother, who stops dancing, mortified. Chelsea raises a hand, in a Native American salute.)

CHELSEA. How.

ETHEL. How'd you get here?

CHELSEA. I rented a car. A [Sebring]. It's made by Chrysler. *(She walks to Ethel. They embrace.)*

ETHEL. You're not supposed to come till the fifteenth.

CHELSEA. Today's the fifteenth.

ETHEL. No!

CHELSEA. 'Fraid so.

ETHEL. Well. No wonder you're here.

CHELSEA. Still have the kid or did you drown him?

ETHEL. Still have him.

CHELSEA. Are he and Norman asleep?

ETHEL. You must be joking. They're out on the lake already, antagonizing the fish. Still have Bill or did you drown him?

CHELSEA. Still got him. But he's not with me. He went back to the coast. He had a mouth that needed looking into.

ETHEL. Oh. You must have left Boston at the crack of dawn.

CHELSEA. I left Boston in the middle of the night. I felt like driving. I didn't feel like getting lost, but it worked out that way.

ETHEL. If you'd come more often, you wouldn't get lost.

CHELSEA. You're right. If I promise to come more often will you give me a cup of coffee?

ETHEL. All right. I could do that. Yes. You must have had a lovely time in Europe. You look wonderful. *(She exits into the kitchen.)*

CHELSEA. I do? I did. I had a lovely time. *(Peers out at the lake.)*

ETHEL. *(Offstage.)* I always thought Norman and I should travel, but we never got to it somehow *(Enters.)* See the boys?

CHELSEA. Yes. What are they doing out there? It's starting to rain.

ETHEL. Ah, well. I told Norman not to go. The loons have been calling for it.

CHELSEA. *(She nods and looks at Ethel.)* Look at you. You've had that robe for as long as I can remember.

ETHEL. *(She tries to arrange it.)* It looks that way, doesn't it?

CHELSEA. It looks great. *(She steps to her and hugs her emphatically, surprising Ethel, who steps back, embarrassed.)*

ETHEL. You're in a huggy mood today. What's the matter?

CHELSEA. You seem different.

ETHEL. You mean old.

CHELSEA. I don't know.

ETHEL. Well, that's what happens if you live long enough: You end up being old. It's one of the disadvantages of a long life. I still prefer it to the alternative. Come sit down. You must be exhausted. *(Ethel sits. Chelsea wanders.)*

CHELSEA. Have Billy and Norman gotten along all right?

ETHEL. Billy is the happiest thing that's happened to Norman since [Roosevelt]. I should have rented him a thirteen-year-old boy years ago.

CHELSEA. You could have traded me in. Billy reminds me of myself out there, way back when. Except I think he makes a better son than I did.

ETHEL. Well, you made a very nice daughter.

CHELSEA. Does Billy put the worm on the hook by himself?

ETHEL. I'm not really sure.

CHELSEA. I hope so. You lose points if you throw up. I remember that. I always apologized to those nice worms before I impaled them. Well, they'll get even with me someday, won't they?

ETHEL. You're beginning to sound an awful lot like your father.

CHELSEA. Uh oh. *(Changing direction.)* Thank you for taking care of Billy.

ETHEL. Thank you. I'm glad it gives us another chance to see you. Plus, it's been a tremendous education. Norman's vocabulary will never be the same.

CHELSEA. *(Turning to the mantel and picking up a picture.)* Look at this: Chelsea on the swim team. That was a great exercise in humiliation.

ETHEL. Oh, stop it. You were a good diver.

CHELSEA. I wasn't a good diver. I was a good sport. I could never do a damn back flip.

ETHEL. Well, we were proud of you for trying.

CHELSEA. Right. Everyone got a big splash out of me trying. Why do you think I subjected myself to all that? I wasn't aiming for the Olympics, you know. I was just trying to please Norman. Because he'd been a diver, in the eighteen hundreds.

ETHEL. Can't you be home for five minutes without getting started on the past?

CHELSEA. This house seems to set me off.

ETHEL. Well, it shouldn't. It's a nice house.

CHELSEA. I act like a big person everywhere else. I do. I'm in charge of Los Angeles. There's just something about coming back here that makes me feel like a little fat girl.

ETHEL. Sit down and tell me about your trip.

CHELSEA. *(An outburst.)* I don't want to sit down. Where were you all that time? You never bailed me out.

ETHEL. I didn't know you needed bailing out.

CHELSEA. Well, I did.

ETHEL. Here we go again. You had a miserable childhood. Your father was overbearing, your mother ignored you. What else is new? Don't you think everyone looks back on her childhood with some bitterness or regret about something? You're a big girl now; aren't you tired of it all? You have this unpleasant chip on your shoulder which is very unattractive. You only come home when I beg you to, and when you get here all you can do is be disagreeable about the past. Life marches on, Chelsea.

CHELSEA. Yeah, your life. In your perfect house on your perfect lake. You don't know what it's like being reminded how worthless you are every time that old son of a bitch crosses your path. *(Ethel suddenly slaps the table [or Chelsea, depending on how brave the actors feel and how "right" it feels in the moment].)*

ETHEL. That old son of a bitch happens to be my husband. *(Chelsea turns away, wiping her eyes. Ethel could just die of remorse.)* I'm sorry. Chelsea. That he's not always kind. It's not … always easy for me either. *(Pause. Trying to lighten the mood.)* You're such a nice person, can't you think of something nice to say?

CHELSEA. No. Oh, yeah: I married Bill in Brussels.

ETHEL. You did what in Brussels?

CHELSEA. I married Bill.

ETHEL. Does it count in this country?

CHELSEA. 'Fraid so.

ETHEL. Well, bless you. Congratulations.

CHELSEA. Thank you.

ETHEL. You have an odd way of building up to good news.

CHELSEA. I know.

ETHEL. Bill seems very nice.

CHELSEA. He's better than nice. He's an adult, too. I decided to go for an adult marriage this time.

ETHEL. Will Billy live with you?

CHELSEA. Yes. That's part of the reason Bill had to get back to L.A. He's murdering his ex-wife. She doesn't want the kid anyway.

ETHEL. Do you?

CHELSEA. Yes.

ETHEL. Well, I'm so pleased.

CHELSEA. Nothing to it. I'm twice as old as you were when you married Norman. Think that means anything?

ETHEL. I hope it means that Bill will be only half as much trouble. Norman will be so surprised.

CHELSEA. I'll bet.

ETHEL. All he wants is for you to be happy.

CHELSEA. Could have fooled me.

ETHEL. Dear God, how long do you plan to keep this up?

CHELSEA. I don't know. Maybe someday we can try to be friends.

ETHEL. Chelsea, Norman is eighty years old. He has heart palpitations and a problem remembering things. When exactly do you expect this friendship to begin? *(Norman arrives on the porch, resembling a wet rooster.)* Norman Thayer, you're soaking wet.

NORMAN. Yes, I know. It's raining. The damn loons are having a good laugh. *(He sees Chelsea.)* Well, well, well. Look at you.

CHELSEA. Hello.

NORMAN. I thought you weren't coming till the fifteenth.

CHELSEA. Today's the fifteenth.

NORMAN. Huh?

ETHEL. 'Fraid so. What have you done with Billy?

NORMAN. He's swimming home. *(Billy slogs onto the porch, lugging the load of gear. He, too, is drenched. Ethel opens the door and he steps in.)*

BILLY. Guess what? It's raining.

ETHEL. Oh, for Lord's sake. Norman, help him with this stuff.

NORMAN. Tsk. *(He walks over and transfers a few items from Billy to the floor.)*

ETHEL. You two need constant supervision, I declare. *(Billy spots Chelsea.)*

BILLY. Hey! Look at you.

CHELSEA. Hey, kid. *(She steps to him and hugs him.)*

BILLY. How ya' doin'?

CHELSEA. Not too shabby.

BILLY. Where's the dentist?

CHELSEA. He went ahead. He's going to call you tonight.

ETHEL. *(Taking Billy by the collar.)* Would you please march upstairs and deposit yourself in a warm shower? Chelsea has news for you which you can't hear till you're dry. *(She prods him up the stairs.)*

NORMAN. What news?

BILLY. *(Turning back.)* Chelsea, you should have seen the bass I caught this morning. *(He holds his hands wide apart.)*

NORMAN. Ha!

BILLY. Five pounds easy.

NORMAN. Ha!

BILLY. But then I saw this depressed look on Norman's face so I decided to let it go.

NORMAN and BILLY. Ha! Ha! Ha! *(Billy exits.)*

ETHEL. Are you two going to be all right alone? I'm sure you can find something to talk about.

NORMAN. Yes. We can talk about the fact that the little person gets to take a shower while I develop pneumonia.

ETHEL. You're a tough old buzzard. Aren't you? *(She exits. Norman scowls after her, then he turns to Chelsea.)*

NORMAN. Tough old buzzard. Don't these little endearments make your heart go pit-a-pat?

CHELSEA. Yes. *(They study each other a moment.)*

NORMAN. Did you hear what the stupid Yankees did?

CHELSEA. No. *(Carefully.)* I don't want to talk about baseball.

NORMAN. Oh. I was just going to mention something you might have found interesting, but it doesn't matter.

CHELSEA. I want to talk about us.

NORMAN. What about us?

CHELSEA. You want to come sit down?

NORMAN. Should I? I've already started a puddle here; perhaps I'd better stand.

CHELSEA. I just wanted to say … that I'm sorry.

NORMAN. Fine. No problem.

CHELSEA. Don't you want to know what I'm sorry about?

NORMAN. I suppose so.

CHELSEA. I'm sorry that our communication has been so bad. That my ... that I've been walking around with a chip on my shoulder. I think it would be a good idea if we tried ... to have the kind of relationship we're supposed to have.

NORMAN. What kind of relationship are we supposed to have?

CHELSEA. Like a father and a daughter.

NORMAN. Ah. Well. Just in the nick of time, huh?

CHELSEA. No.

NORMAN. Worried about the will, are you? I'm leaving everything to you, except what I'm taking with me.

CHELSEA. Stop it. *(She steps to him.)* I don't want anything. We've been mad at each other for too long.

NORMAN. Oh. I didn't realize we were mad. I thought we just didn't like each other. *(Direct hit. Chelsea turns away, hurt. After a moment, she regroups, stepping back to him.)*

CHELSEA. I want to be your friend.

NORMAN. Oh. Okay. Does this mean you're going to come around more often? I may not last eight more years, you know.

CHELSEA. Tsk. I'll come around more often.

NORMAN. Well. It would mean a lot to your mother.

CHELSEA. Okay. *(They look at each other a moment, nothing more to say.)* Now you want to tell me about the Yankees?

NORMAN. The Yankees? They're bums. Your mother said you had some news, what is it?

CHELSEA. I got married in Brussels.

NORMAN. You did? In Brussels. Isn't that nice?

CHELSEA. It is. It's the best thing that's ever happened to me. He makes me very happy.

NORMAN. That's good. He speak English?

CHELSEA. Tsk. I married Bill.

NORMAN. Oh, Bill! That *is* nice.

ETHEL. *(Offstage.)* Next!

NORMAN. What is she screaming about?

CHELSEA. You're next in the shower.

NORMAN. Oh. *(He turns to go. Turns back to Chelsea.)* Talk to you later. *(Chelsea nods, pleased. Ethel appears on the landing.)*

ETHEL. Next!

NORMAN. Good God. This place is starting to sound like a

brothel. *(He climbs the stairs, meeting Ethel midway.)*

ETHEL. What do you know about brothels?

NORMAN. I know a lot about brothels. Brothels is where Chelthea married her thweetheart.

ETHEL. Isn't it wonderful?

NORMAN. Yeth. *(To Chelsea.)* Yes. *(To Ethel.)* Here now, see if you can get us a discount on the dental work. *(He exits. Ethel steps down into the room. She looks at Chelsea, who shrugs. There is the sound of a motorboat.)*

ETHEL. Oh, my goodness. Now here's Charlie. This *is* like a brothel. *(She opens the door.)*

CHELSEA. Charlie! Maybe he'd like to take a shower, too.

ETHEL. Come on up, dear, and have some coffee. Oh, my goodness, the coffee! I'd better get some biscuits. Charlie gets dangerous if you don't feed him. *(She exits into the kitchen. Charlie stomps across the porch in his bright slicker. He calls through the door.)*

CHARLIE. Morning. *(He sees Chelsea and opens the door.)* Well, Holy Mackinoly.

CHELSEA. Hello. What's new?

CHARLIE. *(Laughing.)* It's raining.

CHELSEA. So I've been told. *(Charlie takes off his jacket and hat.)* Look at you. Fat as an old cat.

CHARLIE. Look at you. Chelsea Mackinelsea.

CHELSEA. Charlie Mackinarlie.

CHARLIE. When did you get back?

CHELSEA. This morning.

CHARLIE. Bring the boyfriend?

CHELSEA. No. He's not my boyfriend anymore.

CHARLIE. Oh, no?

CHELSEA. No, I married him.

CHARLIE. What the heck for?

CHELSEA. I felt sorry for him. *(Ethel enters with the coffee and a plate of biscuits.)*

ETHEL. You're early this morning, Charlie. What happened?

CHARLIE. I'm doing the route backwards.

ETHEL. You are?

CHARLIE. Yuh. Thought I'd like to see what it was like. I've been having these little dizzy spells lately, and I thought maybe it was due to going around the lake in the same direction for thirty years.

ETHEL. Are you going to be going backward for the next thirty years, do you think?

CHARLIE. I might. *(The three of them sit.)* Chelsea Mackinelsea tells me she got herself married again.

ETHEL. Yes. Isn't it wonderful?

CHARLIE. I guess. That sort of puts me out of the running again, huh? The old maid mailman.

ETHEL. Oh, pooh. You could have anyone you wanted.

CHARLIE. That's not true, Ethel.

CHELSEA. You wouldn't have wanted me, Charlie. We're too good of friends to be married.

CHARLIE. I guess. Holy Mackinoly. That kid Billy gonna be your son now?

CHELSEA. Yes.

CHARLIE. Huh. Well. Congratulations.

CHELSEA. Thank you.

CHARLIE. How long do you expect to be around this trip?

CHELSEA. Another week.

ETHEL. Good!

CHARLIE. Why don't you come ride the mailboat one time? I'll let you drive it.

CHELSEA. Okay.

CHARLIE. You know, it's funny. I was thinking of you just this morning. I was coming down Koochakiyi Shores, and I almost pulled into the little cove where the big dock used to be, and for a minute there I thought I was a kid again.

ETHEL. There's a lot of that going around, Charlie.

CHARLIE. Yuh? That happen to you, too? *(To Chelsea.)* I can remember so clearly coming in there on my uncle's boat. *The Mariah*, remember? *(Chelsea smiles and nods.)* I'd get up on the deck with that big mail bag for the whole camp, and all those crazy girls would come running down, and I used to feel so important. I'd swing the bag out onto the dock, and then I'd pick up the out-going mail, and somewhere in there, I'd look for you. And you'd always be standing in the back, kind of all alone. And you'd smile at me, and I'd feel like I was the best thing going.

CHELSEA. You were.

CHARLIE. Yuh, I guess I was. Those were the times.

CHELSEA. I remember in the evenings sometimes, you'd come along by Koochakiyi Shores with your brother Tom and anchor your boat and pretend to fish.

CHARLIE. Yuh. We never caught a single one either. We rarely even brought bait. We just liked to hear all you girls sing, and I'd hope to see you. It would start to get dark, and you'd have a camp-fire, and sing those stupid songs.

ETHEL. *(Singing.)* I can see the birds way up in the sky

CHARLIE. *(Overlapping.)* That's one of 'em.

ETHEL. *(Continues singing.)*
    From my tent on the bank of the lake
    At Camp Koochakiyi
    Koochakiyi

CHARLIE. *(He laughs.)* Yuh, yuh, yuh.

CHELSEA. *(Singing.)*
    We are the girls from Camp Koochakiyi
    You can tell who we are
    By the gleam in our eyes.

CHELSEA and ETHEL.
    Our minds are clear and our hearts
    Are strong.
    We are dancing here, but we won't be long.
    There will soon be deer where there now
    Are fawns.

CHARLIE. It was such a sad song. Used to give me the creeps.

CHELSEA and ETHEL.
    But we'll remember our years

ETHEL.
    On Golden Pond.

CHELSEA and ETHEL.
    On Golden Pond.

Scene 2

The middle of September. Late morning.

The room is cluttered again. The tables are back in from the porch, the dust covers are back in place, the dining chairs piled upside down on the oak table. Outside, the sky is bright and blue.

After a moment, Ethel enters from the kitchen, carrying a cardboard box. She sets it down on a table, and goes back into the kitchen. She wears a tidy pantsuit now.

Norman comes in the downstage left door. He is dressed in his "traveling clothes," neat slacks and a jacket. He sees the box and picks it up. He holds it, looking about the room. He wanders up to the platform, and sets the box down. He examines his fishing gear quickly, and then walks up the stairs and into the hallway above.

Ethel comes back into the room with another box. She begins to set it down, realizes the first is gone, looks for it. She sees it on the platform and stares at it, puzzled. She sets down the second box and then goes up the steps for the first, which she carries back down, and then out the downstage door.

Norman comes down the stairs, carrying a fishing pole. He leans it against the couch. He spots the box Ethel has left, which looks very much like the one he just moved. He begins to carry it out, when he thinks of something and sets the box down where he left the first one. He goes to the hat rack and studies the collection. Ethel returns.

ETHEL. Norman, what in the world are you doing with the boxes?
NORMAN. Nothing. Which one of these hats is your favorite?
ETHEL. You moved this box and you moved the other box, too. Are we moving out or in?

NORMAN. Oh. That box. I'm carrying that box to the car. I'm helping you.

ETHEL. You certainly have a roundabout way of doing it. The car is in the back, you know.

NORMAN. I know. Which hat is your favorite?

ETHEL. I dislike them all equally. *(She carries the box downstage.)*

NORMAN. *I* was going to take that box.

ETHEL. Yes. It's where you were going to take it that had me concerned, so I'm taking it myself. *(Stopping by the fireplace.)* What is your old fish pole doing here?

NORMAN. I fixed it. I fixed the reel, and I retied the splints.

ETHEL. What's it doing here?

NORMAN. It's waiting to go to the car. I'm going to mail it to Billy.

ETHEL. What? You can't mail a fish pole.

NORMAN. Of course I can. I'm a taxpayer. He may want to go fishing. I assume they have fish in California.

ETHEL. Well ... *(She looks up. Norman is now wearing on of the floppy hats.)* What are you doing with that terrible hat?

NORMAN. *(Crossing down.)* I'm mailing it to Billy with the fish pole. You can't fish without a hat.

ETHEL. He tries fishing with that thing on his head anywhere outside of Golden Pond, he'll probably be arrested.

NORMAN. Not in California he won't.

ETHEL. Well, bring it then. There's barely room. *(She carries out the box, but Norman lingers. He wanders to the bookshelves and studies the books. He pulls one down and sits, starting to read. The phone rings and he glances up but ignores it. Ethel steps back in.)* Did you get lost?

NORMAN. No, I'm over here. *(The phone rings again.)* The phone's ringing.

ETHEL. Well, what do you know? I suppose we'd better answer it.

NORMAN. Yes. *(She steps to the phone and picks it up.)*

ETHEL. Hello?

BILL. Is this Paradise, Maine?

ETHEL. Hello?

BILL. Hello. Ethel. How are you?

ETHEL. I'm fine, thank you. How are you?

BILL. Couldn't be better.

ETHEL. Good.

BILL. We weren't sure if you'd still be there.

ETHEL. We're leaving right now.

BILL. Well, you drive safely.

ETHEL. Thank you.

NORMAN. Who is it?

ETHEL. *(Covering the receiver.)* I have no idea. *(Into the phone.)* Who is this?

BILL. Bill. Your son-in-law.

ETHEL. Oh, Bill! How are you?

BILL. We're doing great.

ETHEL. Good. *(To Norman.)* It's Bill.

NORMAN. Bill? Oh. Bill!

BILL. You have a good trip, okay?

ETHEL. Thank you, Bill.

BILL. How about coming to California?

ETHEL. Well, we'd love to.

BILL. Want to talk to my girl?

ETHEL. Yes, Of course, put her on.

CHELSEA. Hello, mommy.

ETHEL. Hi, darling.

CHELSEA. Hitting the road?

ETHEL. Yes. We're just leaving. Two more boxes and say goodbye to the lake and that will be that.

CHELSEA. It seems early to be going.

ETHEL. Oh, no. Everybody else is gone practically.

CHELSEA. Well, it's always summer out here.

ETHEL. Your house sounds wonderful. Send us some pictures.

CHELSEA. Just come and see it in person, save me the postage.

ETHEL. We would love to, dear. Maybe in January.

CHELSEA. Would you come here, really?

ETHEL. Instead of Florida, yes. We'll discuss it.

CHELSEA. Good.

ETHEL. If I can get Norman to accept the fact that Los Angeles is part of the United States, it shouldn't be too much trouble. He's still convinced you need a passport to get out there.

CHELSEA. Let me talk to him.

ETHEL. Of course. I'll get him. Norman, she wants to talk to you.

NORMAN. I've just started my book.

ETHEL. Norman, she wants to talk to you.

NORMAN. Why would she want to talk to me?

ETHEL. Get it in gear, Norman. *(He stands. Ethel speaks into the phone cheerily.)* He's coming, dear. Give my love to Billy. We hope to see you soon.

CHELSEA. Don't hope, just come.

ETHEL. Yes. Bye. *(Norman flings his book onto the couch and Ethel hands him the phone.)*

NORMAN. What will I say to her?

ETHEL. You'll think of something.

NORMAN. *(Into the phone.)* Hello. Who is this?

CHELSEA. It's your kid. Chelsea. Remember?

NORMAN. Oh, how are you?

CHELSEA. Not bad.

NORMAN. Oh. How nice. How's the weather? No earthquakes? *(Ethel shakes her head. She picks up the fishing pole, and takes the hat off Norman's head. She carries them both outside.)*

CHELSEA. We don't have earthquakes every day.

NORMAN. Good.

CHELSEA. You should come see for yourself. It's pretty nice.

NORMAN. Oh, I don't know if we'll be able to go all the way out there. Ethel's health isn't what it could be, you know.

CHELSEA. Is there something I should be worried about?

NORMAN. No, nothing serious. She's just more ornery than usual.

CHELSEA. Wouldn't have anything to do with you, would it?

NORMAN. Oh, no, I'm in great form myself. Just a lot of pain. Nothing to worry about.

CHELSEA. And you're coming to California.

NORMAN. Well, we'll certainly consider it.

CHELSEA. No. I want you to come.

NORMAN. Oh, thank you.

CHELSEA. Because I love you.

NORMAN. Oh, well. I love you, too. *(He's embarrassed.)*

CHELSEA. See how much easier that is than gallbladder surgery?

NORMAN. Yes. *(Brightly.)* Billy there?

CHELSEA. Yes. Billy's here.

NORMAN. Good. Could I speak to him?

CHELSEA. You got him. You two have fun in Wilmington. Okay?

NORMAN. Yes, we will. You have fun, too — the three of you.

CHELSEA. Okay. And call me.

NORMAN. Okay, Chelsea. Bye. *(He stares off while waiting for Billy to answer.)*

BILLY. This the old man of the sea?

NORMAN. Hello, cool breeze. How's the chicks?

BILLY. The chicks are fine. How's the fish?

NORMAN. The fish are all gone, somewhere.

BILLY. Well, where'd they go?

NORMAN. I don't know. They go to sleep, I believe. How's your reading?

BILLY. I'm halfway into *The Count of Monte Cristo*.

NORMAN. Don't tell me! How wonderful.

BILLY. Yeah, it ain't bad. Alexander Dumb-ass, you know.

NORMAN. Yes, I know, but it's pronounced Doo-ma, not Dumbass. Say that. Doo-ma.

BILLY. Doo-ma.

NORMAN. Tres bien.

BILLY. Merci. And au revoir. I've gotta go, sorry.

NORMAN. That's okay, run along. I expect you'll want to do a little cruising on your way to school.

BILLY. Tell Ethel to send me some Toll House cookies. Chelsea tries, but, you know, it ain't the same.

NORMAN. I'll tell her.

BILLY. And you hang loose, okay? 'Cause I kinda miss you, dude.

NORMAN. Well, I miss you, too.

BILLY. Okay. Cool.

NORMAN. Listen, Ethel and I are coming out to visit, you know.

BILLY. Get out of town. For real?

NORMAN. Oh, yes. In the winter.

BILLY. Don't bullshit me, man.

NORMAN. I'm not bullshitting you.

BILLY. Well, that would be very cool. I would like that.

NORMAN. Yes. Me, too. Bye! Adieu, mon vieux. *(He hangs up, feeling quite chipper. Ethel enters.)* I talked to Billy.

ETHEL. How nice.

NORMAN. He said he wants you to mail him some Toll House cookies.

ETHEL. Oh, he does, does he?

NORMAN. Yes. He said Chelsea makes them but they're not as good.

ETHEL. Huh. Well, that's the way it is with us grandmothers, you know. Chelsea mention us going out there for a visit?

NORMAN. I think she did.

ETHEL. I guess we could, don't you think?

NORMAN. Well … I guess so.

ETHEL. I think they're going to make a go of it.

NORMAN. What do you mean?

ETHEL. The marriage. I think it's a success.

NORMAN. It's lasted over a month already.

61

ETHEL. It makes me feel so good to think that Chelsea is finally settling down.

NORMAN. Yes. Want to play a quick game of Parcheesi? Loser drives.

ETHEL. No. Haven't you been humiliated enough? You owe me four million dollars.

NORMAN. Double or nothing?

ETHEL. When we get home, Norman. We've got the whole winter ahead of us.

NORMAN. Yes.

ETHEL. Come on, let's get the other boxes, and be gone. *(She heads into the kitchen. Norman stays where he is, looking about. Ethel calls from offstage.)* Norman!

NORMAN. Yes

ETHEL. Would you come here? *(He crosses to the kitchen door.)*

NORMAN. What is it? *(He exits.)*

ETHEL. *(Offstage.)* Get the last box, if it's not too heavy. *(She enters, carrying a box.)*

NORMAN. Of course it's not too heavy. Good God, this is heavy!

ETHEL. Well, wait and I'll help you with it then.

NORMAN. *(Offstage.)* You're trying to kill me.

ETHEL. I've thought about it. *(She carries her box downstage as he comes out with his. He crosses to the platform. She waits for him at the door. He moves slowly.)*

NORMAN. Whatever have you got in here?

ETHEL. My mother's china. I've decided to take it to Wilmington and use it there.

NORMAN. Good God.

ETHEL. Are you all right?

NORMAN. Yes. Your mother never liked me.

ETHEL. Oh, stop. She loved you.

NORMAN. Then why did she have such heavy china?

ETHEL. Set it back down if it's too much trouble.

NORMAN. I don't want to break your mother's china. Ouch.

ETHEL. Norman! Put the box down! *(He drops his box, which crashes to the floor. Ethel sets down her box as Norman crumples, clutching his chest. She runs to him as he sags to his knees. She helps him lie down, frightened now.)* Where's your medicine? I'm afraid it's in the car. Oh, God. *(She runs to the door and exits. Norman lies still, gasping for breath, in pain. Ethel runs back in with his pill bottle. She kneels by him, struggling to open the bottle.)* Here, take this and put it under your tongue. *(She holds out a pill.)*

NORMAN. What is it?

ETHEL. Nitroglycerin. Put it under your tongue.

NORMAN. You must be mad. I'll blow up.

ETHEL. Do it! *(Norman takes the pill. She kneels beside him, watching. He breathes deeply and leans his head back, his eyes closed. Ethel begins to weep.)* Norman? Norman!

NORMAN. *(His eyes closed.)* Maybe you'd better call a doctor.

ETHEL. Oh, yes! *(She jumps up.)* Dear God. *(She rushes to the phone and dials "O.")* Hello, hello. Dear God. How are you feeling, Norman?

NORMAN. Oh, pretty good. How are you?

ETHEL. Is the medicine doing anything?

NORMAN. No.

ETHEL. Why don't they answer the phone?

NORMAN. Whom did you call?

ETHEL. The stupid operator. *(Into the receiver.)* Hello? Hello! I'm going to have to call the hospital directly. *(She hangs up and pulls out the phone book, thumbing through it frantically.)* Hospital, hospital.

NORMAN. Ethel …

ETHEL. *(Fearing the worst.)* What is it?

NORMAN. Come here. *(Ethel drops the phone book.)*

ETHEL. Oh, God. *(She rushes over and kneels by his side.)* Yes, Norman.

NORMAN. Ethel.

ETHEL. *(Crying.)* Yes. I'm here.

NORMAN. I think I feel all right now.

ETHEL. Are you serious?

NORMAN. I think so. My heart's stopped hurting. Maybe I'm dead.

ETHEL. It really doesn't hurt?

NORMAN. Really doesn't. Shall I dance to prove it?

ETHEL. *(Falling against him.)* Oh, Norman. Oh, thank God. I love you so much. *(She cries.)*

NORMAN. Now my heart's starting to hurt again. Sorry about your mother's china.

ETHEL. Why did you strain yourself? You know better.

NORMAN. I was showing off. Trying to turn you on.

ETHEL. Well, you succeeded. There's no need for you to try that sort of thing again.

NORMAN. Good. *(They sit quietly for a moment.)*

ETHEL. What if we never leave? What if we just stay here and let the leaves fall and the winter come across the lake?

NORMAN. Okay. Then Charlie can find our bodies in the spring.

ETHEL. Then we'll take it with us. We'll pack up the lake and the house and everything and every … thing and put it in a suitcase and take it home.

NORMAN. Okay, but you're carrying it.

ETHEL. Norman. *(A pause.)* This was the first time I've really felt we were going to die.

NORMAN. I've known it all along.

ETHEL. Yes, I know. But when I looked at you across the room, I could really see you dead. I could see you in your blue suit and a white starched shirt, lying in Thomas's Funeral Parlor on Bradshaw Street.

NORMAN. How did I look?

ETHEL. Not good, Norman. *(Pause.)* You've been talking about dying ever since I met you. It's been your favorite topic of conversation. And I've *had* to think about it. Our parents, my sister and brother, your brother, their wives, our dearest friends, practically everyone from the old days on Golden Pond, all dead. I've seen death, and touched death, and feared it. But today was the first time I've felt it.

NORMAN. How does it feel?

ETHEL. Odd, I guess. But not that bad, really. Almost comforting, not so frightening, not such a bad place to go. I don't know.

NORMAN. *(He nods, affected by her little poem.)* Want to see if you can find my book?

ETHEL. Here it is. *(She finds it on the couch.)* Going to take it?

NORMAN. Nope. It belongs here. Put it on the shelf. *(She crosses and returns the book to its place.)* I'll read it next year.

ETHEL. Yes. Next year. *(She wanders around behind the couch.)* We'll have the whole summer to read and pick berries and play Monopoly, and Billy can come for as long as he likes, and you two can fish, and I'll make cookies, and life will go on, won't it?

NORMAN. I hope so.

ETHEL. This is my favorite time of year on Golden Pond. No bugs.

NORMAN. Nope.

ETHEL. I guess I'll go down and say goodbye to the lake. Feel like coming?

NORMAN. Yes. *(He rises slowly.)*

ETHEL. You sure you're strong enough?

NORMAN. I think so. If I fall over face first in the water, you'll know I wasn't.

ETHEL. *(Waiting for him.)* Well, go easy, for God's sake.

NORMAN. *(Finally standing and facing her.)* Hello, there.

ETHEL. Hi.

NORMAN. *(Taking her in his arms.)* Want to dance? Or would you rather just suck face?

ETHEL. You really are a case, you know. *(Call of a loon.)* My word, Norman, the loons. They've come round to say goodbye.

NORMAN. How nice.

ETHEL. Just the two of them now. Little baby's grown up and moved to Los Angeles or somewhere.

NORMAN. Yes. *(They kiss. A long, gentle moment passes. They look at each other, and then look away.)*

ETHEL. Well, let's go down. *(They exit. He follows her across the porch and down the steps.)* Hello, Golden Pond. We've come to say goodbye.

End of Play

PROPERTY LIST

Basket of branches
Furniture dust covers
Dust cloth
Rack of hats with old straw hat and floppy red fishing hat
Small mirror
Wooden doll
Telephone
Photos on mantel of family life
Books: *Swiss Family Robinson, A Connecticut Yankee in King Arthur's Court*
Binoculars hanging from hook
Footstool
Newspaper, classified ads
2 buckets of strawberries
Pile of newspapers
Small package
Several letters
Rolled newspaper
Carafe of coffee
Plate of biscuits
Glass of milk
Larger package
Poster: "Welcome Home, Chelsea"
2 suitcases
Packages of gifts
Tackle box
2 fishing poles
Fishnet
Bait can
Boat cushions
Coil of rope
Umbrella
Bag of cookies
Leaf rake
Larger bag containing cookies, biscuits, 2 sandwiches, thermos of milk, jar of raspberries
Daddy longlegs or bug on mantle
3 large cardboard boxes
Small jar of medicine (pills)

SOUND EFFECTS

Phone ringing
Motorboat
Call of a loon
Car pulling into driveway
Footsteps (3 people)
Boat horn

On Golden Pond Camp Song

Music by Dan Moses Schreier
Lyrics by Ernest Thompson

Moderato (♩ = c. 108)

Vocals

I Can See The Birds, Way Up In The Sky, From My Tent

On The Bank Of The Lake At Camp

Koo cha ki yi (STOMP) Koo cha ki yi. (STOMP)

I Can See The Trees And The Hills Be – yond,

From My Tent On The Bank Of The Lake

Called Go – old – en Pond, On Go – old – en Pond

We Are The Girls From Camp Koo cha ki yi,

You Can Tell Who We Are By The Gleam

In Our Eyes. Our Minds Are Clear And Our

On Golden Pond Camp Song

Hearts Are Strong. We Are Dan – cing Here, But We
Won't Be Long. There Will Soon Be Deer Where There
Now Are Fawns. But We'll Re – mem-ber Our Years
On Go-old-en Pond, (STOMP) On Go-old-en Pond. (STOMP)

ON GOLDEN POND
Set Design by Steven Rubin

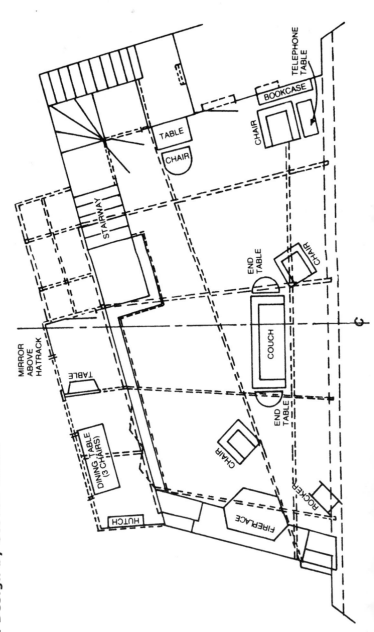

NEW PLAYS

★ **BENGAL TIGER AT THE BAGHDAD ZOO by Rajiv Joseph.** The lives of two American Marines and an Iraqi translator are forever changed by an encounter with a quick-witted tiger who haunts the streets of war-torn Baghdad. "[A] boldly imagined, harrowing and surprisingly funny drama." –*NY Times.* "Tragic yet darkly comic and highly imaginative." –*CurtainUp.* [5M, 2W] ISBN: 978-0-8222-2565-2

★ **THE PITMEN PAINTERS by Lee Hall, inspired by a book by William Feaver.** Based on the triumphant true story, a group of British miners discover a new way to express themselves and unexpectedly become art-world sensations. "Excitingly ambiguous, in-the-moment theater." –*NY Times.* "Heartfelt, moving and deeply politicized." –*Chicago Tribune.* [5M, 2W] ISBN: 978-0-8222-2507-2

★ **RELATIVELY SPEAKING by Ethan Coen, Elaine May and Woody Allen.** In TALKING CURE, Ethan Coen uncovers the sort of insanity that can only come from family. Elaine May explores the hilarity of passing in GEORGE IS DEAD. In HONEYMOON MOTEL, Woody Allen invites you to the sort of wedding day you won't forget. "Firecracker funny." –*NY Times.* "A rollicking good time." –*New Yorker.* [8M, 7W] ISBN: 978-0-8222-2394-8

★ **SONS OF THE PROPHET by Stephen Karam.** If to live is to suffer, then Joseph Douaihy is more alive than most. With unexplained chronic pain and the fate of his reeling family on his shoulders, Joseph's health, sanity, and insurance premium are on the line. "Explosively funny." –*NY Times.* "At once deep, deft and beautifully made." –*New Yorker.* [5M, 3W] ISBN: 978-0-8222-2597-3

★ **THE MOUNTAINTOP by Katori Hall.** A gripping reimagination of events the night before the assassination of the civil rights leader Dr. Martin Luther King, Jr. "An ominous electricity crackles through the opening moments." –*NY Times.* "[A] thrilling, wild, provocative flight of magical realism." –*Associated Press.* "Crackles with theatricality and a humanity more moving than sainthood." –*NY Newsday.* [1M, 1W] ISBN: 978-0-8222-2603-1

★ **ALL NEW PEOPLE by Zach Braff.** Charlie is 35, heartbroken, and just wants some time away from the rest of the world. Long Beach Island seems to be the perfect escape until his solitude is interrupted by a motley parade of misfits who show up and change his plans. "Consistently and sometimes sensationally funny." –*NY Times.* "A morbidly funny play about the trendy new existential condition of being young, adorable, and miserable." –*Variety.* [2M, 2W] ISBN: 978-0-8222-2562-1

DRAMATISTS PLAY SERVICE, INC.
440 Park Avenue South, New York, NY 10016 212-683-8960 Fax 212-213-1539
postmaster@dramatists.com   www.dramatists.com

NEW PLAYS

★ **CLYBOURNE PARK by Bruce Norris.** WINNER OF THE 2011 PULITZER PRIZE AND 2012 TONY AWARD. Act One takes place in 1959 as community leaders try to stop the sale of a home to a black family. Act Two is set in the same house in the present day as the now predominantly African-American neighborhood battles to hold its ground. "Vital, sharp-witted and ferociously smart." –*NY Times.* "A theatrical treasure…Indisputably, uproariously funny." –*Entertainment Weekly.* [4M, 3W] ISBN: 978-0-8222-2697-0

★ **WATER BY THE SPOONFUL by Quiara Alegría Hudes.** WINNER OF THE 2012 PULITZER PRIZE. A Puerto Rican veteran is surrounded by the North Philadelphia demons he tried to escape in the service. "This is a very funny, warm, and yes uplifting play." –*Hartford Courant.* "The play is a combination poem, prayer and app on how to cope in an age of uncertainty, speed and chaos." –*Variety.* [4M, 3W] ISBN: 978-0-8222-2716-8

★ **RED by John Logan.** WINNER OF THE 2010 TONY AWARD. Mark Rothko has just landed the biggest commission in the history of modern art. But when his young assistant, Ken, gains the confidence to challenge him, Rothko faces the agonizing possibility that his crowning achievement could also become his undoing. "Intense and exciting." –*NY Times.* "Smart, eloquent entertainment." –*New Yorker.* [2M] ISBN: 978-0-8222-2483-9

★ **VENUS IN FUR by David Ives.** Thomas, a beleaguered playwright/director, is desperate to find an actress to play Vanda, the female lead in his adaptation of the classic sadomasochistic tale *Venus in Fur.* "Ninety minutes of good, kinky fun." –*NY Times.* "A fast-paced journey into one man's entrapment by a clever, vengeful female." –*Associated Press.* [1M, 1W] ISBN: 978-0-8222-2603-1

★ **OTHER DESERT CITIES by Jon Robin Baitz.** Brooke returns home to Palm Springs after a six-year absence and announces that she is about to publish a memoir dredging up a pivotal and tragic event in the family's history—a wound they don't want reopened. "Leaves you feeling both moved and gratifyingly sated." –*NY Times.* "A genuine pleasure." –*NY Post.* [2M, 3W] ISBN: 978-0-8222-2605-5

★ **TRIBES by Nina Raine.** Billy was born deaf into a hearing family and adapts brilliantly to his family's unconventional ways, but it's not until he meets Sylvia, a young woman on the brink of deafness, that he finally understands what it means to be understood. "A smart, lively play." –*NY Times.* "[A] bright and boldly provocative drama." –*Associated Press.* [3M, 2W] ISBN: 978-0-8222-2751-9

DRAMATISTS PLAY SERVICE, INC.
440 Park Avenue South, New York, NY 10016 212-683-8960 Fax 212-213-1539
postmaster@dramatists.com www.dramatists.com